THE COLLEGES
AND THE COURTS
1946-50

THE COLLEGES AND THE COURTS 1946-50

Judicial Decisions Regarding Higher Education in the United States

By M. M. CHAMBERS

WITH A FOREWORD BY
EDWARD C. ELLIOTT

COLUMBIA UNIVERSITY PRESS
NEW YORK 1952

This publication was made possible by funds granted by Carnegie Corporation of New York to Carnegie Foundation for the Advancement of Teaching. The Corporation and the Foundation are not, however, the authors or publishers of this publication and are not to be understood as approving by virtue of this grant any of the statements made or views expressed therein.

PUBLISHED IN GREAT BRITAIN, CANADA, AND INDIA
BY GEOFFREY CUMBERLEGE, OXFORD UNIVERSITY PRESS
LONDON, TORONTO, AND BOMBAY

MANUFACTURED IN THE UNITED STATES OF AMERICA

FOREWORD

FOR the third time since the publication of *The Colleges and the Courts* in 1936, Dr. M. M. Chambers has assembled, analyzed, and interpreted, for a five-year period, the numerous judicial decisions relating to institutions of higher education in the United States. Thus, he continues his long recognized contributions to this distinctive and increasingly important factor of the administration of American education.

The records of the litigation brought together in the present volume provide proof of the never-ending problem of adjusting the scope, controls, and operations of our colleges and universities to the complicated and changing conditions of modern democratic life. This problem is well illustrated by Dr. Chambers in his initial statement of the trends of 1946–50.

It is well to keep in mind the organizational character of American higher education, existing as it does within the legal framework of forty-eight states; and also the tenuous relationship of the National Government. Disregarding the local, as contrasted to the general, significance of many of the issues involved, there appears to be a growing tendency to appeal to the courts for the adjudication of controverted causes.

The original study of 1936, covering the period of the century and a quarter since the famous Dartmouth College decision of 1819, cited 962 cases—United States Supreme Court, Federal Courts, and State Courts. In the second study (1936–40) 145 cases are referred to; and 193 in the third study (1941–45). The present volume gives consideration to 190 cases.

All students of contemporary higher education will recognize the timely service of the Carnegie Corporation of New York in making readily available the material of this publication. Thereby will be further understanding of the ways that things come to be as they are. "The acts of today become the precedents of tomorrow."

EDWARD C. ELLIOTT
President Emeritus, Purdue University

Lafayette, Indiana
December, 1951

PREFACE

COVERING decisions of the higher State and Federal courts during the five years 1946–50 in cases affecting universities and colleges in the United States, this volume is the fourth of a series.

The basic volume, *The Colleges and the Courts,* published in 1936, carried the story from the early nineteenth century through 1935. Since then there have been supplementary volumes at quinquennial intervals, bearing the same title, with indication of the years covered: 1936–40, 1941–45, and 1946–50.

The first three units in the series are now out of print, but copies are accessible in all parts of the country in university and public libraries, law libraries, and in the offices of many college and university presidents and business managers.

The arrangement of the contents within each of the four volumes is substantially similar, but not precisely identical. A few of the chapters and parts of chapters which follow have appeared previously under my name, either in the *Educational Record* (American Council on Education, Washington, D.C.), or in *College and University Business* (Modern Hospitals Publishing Co., Inc., Chicago), and to their publishers I am indebted for permission to revise, reorganize, and incorporate such materials. To the university and college presidents and business officers who have aided me orally and by correspondence my thanks also go.

M. M. CHAMBERS

December, 1951

CONTENTS

PART FOUR

Fiscal Relationships with Governmental Units

PART FIVE

Financial Support from Private Sources, Institutional Property, Other Matters

THE COLLEGES AND THE COURTS
1946-50

INTRODUCTION

SOME TRENDS OF 1946–50

THESE are the years which saw college and university enrollments shoot upward to unprecedented peaks, due in large part to the influx of slightly overage veterans of World War II whose education had been delayed. Every campus had its colony of young wives and babies come to live with the husbands and fathers who were students. Many a child was born and lived his first years at a university. A somewhat amusing and not altogether unimportant by-product of this aspect of college life was a fresh consideration of the old question of the voting residence of students. "These students are family men, not college boys away from their parental homes," said a New York judge. "These petitioners have shown their eligibility to vote from the only residences they have."

The pressure upon housing facilities gave new impetus to methods of financing self-liquidating dormitories. In at least one instance the bonds issued for this purpose by a state university were approved by the state supreme court and the transaction sustained although it had been executed without authorization by state statute; and this in Missouri, a state whose state university has not been regarded as having any large degree of constitutional independence. After reviewing the record as to the campus housing stringency, and noting that the Curators of the University of Missouri had no express power to issue bonds, the court concluded, "Have they the implied power? We are convinced they have in this instance."

CRACKS IN THE WALL OF RACIAL SEGREGATION

Four decisions of the United States Supreme Court during this period did much to elaborate, implement, and effectuate the principle declared by Mr. Chief Justice Hughes in the *Gaines Case* of 1938; namely, that a state is obligated to provide within its own borders, for qualified Negro applicants, facilities for graduate and professional education substantially equal to those afforded for white students. In rapid succession during the years 1948–50 the nation's highest tribunal decided cases in which it declared that delay in providing the required facilities can not be countenanced; that a small, newly established, segregated graduate or professional school for Negroes can not be the substantial equivalent of a long-established, reputable, and well-equipped school of the same kind in a state university; and that when a state university admits a qualified Negro graduate or professional student, it can not lawfully segregate him within the university by restricting his choice of seats in classroom, library, or cafeteria, but must accord him the same treatment as it accords students of other races.

Under the reasoning of these decisions and their forerunners in inferior federal courts, several Southern state universities have begun the practice of admitting Negroes to their graduate and professional schools, so that the *Gaines* decision of a dozen years ago at last begins to bear fruit.

The principle is strictly adhered to in a Maryland Court of Appeals decision of 1950 ordering the University of Maryland to act upon the application of a Negro girl for admission to its school of nursing, notwithstanding the fact that she had declined an offer by the state to afford her nursing education facilities not merely equal, but admittedly superior, at Meharry Medical College in Nashville, and at no greater total cost to herself. This would have been accomplished under the interstate compact to which Maryland is a party, and which is administered by the body known as the Board of Control for Southern Regional Education. The Maryland court assumed, but did not decide, that the compact is valid, though it has not had the consent of Congress; because resolving that issue was not necessary to the decision in this case. The Supreme Court of the United States declined to review the case on *certiorari.*

LIMITS OF STATE LICENSING POWER

Two sections of the New York Education Law relating to the authority of the Board of Regents of the University of the State of New York to regulate private schools were declared unconstitutional by state courts in 1948 and 1950. In the one instance, a statute empowering the Regents to regulate the operation of elementary or lower schools by any persons or corporations other than public school authorities or established religious groups was struck down by a divided vote of the Court of Appeals, because it contained no statutory guide for the exercise of the Regents' discretion, and was therefore held to be an unconstitutional delegation of legislative power.

In the other case, the majority of a divided Appellate Division decided that a statute empowering the Commissioner of Education to approve the tuition fees charged by trade schools, as a prerequisite to their licensing by the Board of Regents, can not stand because it authorizes "price-fixing"—a sphere in which, said the court somewhat surprisingly, the public has no proper concern. It seems quite possible that a different view might be taken if and when the case goes up to the Court of Appeals.

THE STATUS OF STATE INSTITUTIONS

The relation between the state legislative power and a state university or system of higher education which has prerogatives derived from the state constitution continued to be a center of litigation. A popularly initiated statute of Arizona which would have placed nonteaching employees of the state university and the state colleges under a state civil service system was declared invalid as conflicting with the constitutional authority of the Board of Regents of the University and State Colleges to select and supervise its own employees. A Nevada act of 1947 was invalidated by the highest court of the state because it would have created an advisory board to the Board of Regents of the University of Nevada. In the view of the majority of the court, the Board of Regents, owing its existence to the constitution of the state, must be supreme within its own sphere, and the legislature can not create any other body to share or assist in its constitutional duties.

Michigan State College, long known as possessing a high degree of constitutional independence, nevertheless is held to be compulsorily covered by the Workmen's Compensation Act, because this act is an exercise of the state's police power—an area in which the legislature is paramount. So difficult was this decision for the Michigan supreme court that the conclusion was determined by vote of four justices against four, in which event, by a species of default, the judgment of the lower court is automatically affirmed.

The Board of Regents of the University System of Georgia was judicially sustained in its right to operate a low-cost laundry and dry-cleaning service for students and other persons connected with an institution under its control, as against the contentions of local commercial competitors alleging that this invaded their rights. Likewise, the same service may be lawfully operated by an institutional athletic association which is a nonprofit corporation, under contract with the Regents.

THE TAX CASES

As to the tests of exemption from property taxes, an interesting development was a break in the line of decisions in Ohio which have in recent years seemed to establish the astonishing proposition that an institution can not be charitable within the meaning of the exemption clauses unless it is open to the public generally—i.e., a theological school open only to members of a particular religious denomination can not be exempt under this interpretation of Ohio statutes. In 1949 this doctrine was openly questioned by two of the justices of the Ohio supreme court who voted with the majority of the court in holding a Bible college entitled to exemption. It is possible that the outspoken challenge of the two justices may signalize the return of the pendulum to a less extreme position.

In two other states recent decisions reveal continued adherence to principles which are probably obsolescent. Texas uses the test of exclusive use for school purposes, with no distinction between nonprofit and proprietary schools. Michigan likewise apparently disregards the question of nonprofit versus proprietary character when dealing with private schools, and distinguishes instead between academic schools and vocational schools. Thus a 1948 decision holds a nonprofit business college taxable, while in earlier decision held a proprietary academic preparatory school exempt.

PURCHASE AND "LEASE-BACK" OF COMMERCIAL PROPERTY

Problems arise in the application of the federal income tax to a business corporation which sells a commercial or industrial plant to a nonprofit educational institution at a nominal price and simultaneously obtains a long-term lease of the plant; and then treats the difference between the book value of the plant and the sale price as a deductible loss in computing its income tax for the year in which the transaction took place. A 1950 decision of the United States Tax Court holds that in fact the transaction is not a sale, but is an *exchange* of the title to the plant for the long-term leasehold. Holding that the claimed deductible loss on the cash sale could therefore not be deducted in computing the tax for the current year, the court decided that the claimed loss would be properly allowable as depreciation on the leasehold, spread over the full period of the lease. This attenuates the tax advantage to the seller.

To what extent transactions such as the foregoing are merely ingenious and legitimate methods of obtaining higher returns on endowment funds for educational institutions, and to what extent, if any, they are devices to obtain by collusion tax advantages for the participating business corporations contrary to the intent of Congress, are questions likely to receive recurrent attention in the federal courts, as well as in the national legislative body where amendments to the Internal Revenue Code are proposed from time to time.

EDUCATIONAL TRUST FUNDS

The modern tendency of the courts of equity to sustain the validity of charitable trusts as against allegations of uncertainty in the terms of the trust instrument continues. The spirit of this trend is exemplified in the words of the New Jersey Court of Chancery in a 1948 decision: "If the intention be charity, the court will execute the instrument, however vaguely the donor may have indicated his purpose."

Thus it is not uncommon for a trust to be upheld when the instrument contains little more than a statement of charitable intent, and leaves the selection of specific purposes and the defining of classes of beneficiaries entirely to the trustee. Furthermore, some states provide by statute that no charitable trust otherwise valid shall fail for want of a trustee; and so if the instrument designates a trustee legally incompetent to accept the trust, or fails to designate any trustee at all, it becomes the duty of the court of equity to appoint a suitable trustee and exercise a general superintendence over the execution of the trust.

These trends regarding the validity of charitable trusts are of consequence to colleges and universities because, for one reason, they promise eventually to bring some clarification into confused corners of the law concerning gifts to educational institutions. For example, an Indiana court in 1947 declared that a deferred gift to a charitable corporation for its charitable purposes, without further restrictions, was not an outright or absolute gift, but created a trust which would survive the disappearance of the original donee by merger with another charitable corporation. The principle is very well put in the words of the Tennessee supreme court, when it said forty-five years ago:

A corporation organized for charitable purposes has these purposes and trusts set out in its charter and articles of foundation, so that the trusts are thus made certain and will control; due deference being paid to the directions of the testator, if any are given. But no trusts in such case need be declared, as they are set out in the charter and articles of foundation.

In other words, all assets of a nonprofit charitable institution are held in trust in a broad general sense for its charitable purposes. To be sure, not all are in the form of permanent endowment, and not all are unrestricted as to purpose. A gift for designated restricted purposes, when accepted, creates an active special trust governed by the terms of the gift; and an unrestricted gift, or an asset of the institution acquired in some other manner, though it may not create any explicit special trust, may come to be said to fall into the general trust framework created by the corporate charter of the institution as an organization for charitable purposes.

There is a tendency to apply the judicial doctrine of *cy pres* freely to insure the execution of a charitable trust in cases where it would otherwise be defeated. Out of many recent examples, one is that of a testator who bequeathed a mass of unintelligible and irrational typed notes and a fund of $150,000 to complete and publish his researches as represented therein. The will directed that the bequest be offered successively to seven named institutions and associations, of which Princeton University was one. All the offerees rejected the gift, but Princeton University argued that this was a case for *cy pres,* and that the gift should go to the Princeton department of philosophy as an endowment for philosophical research. This argument was the basis of the decision of the New Jersey Court of Chancery. The will contained ample evidences of a general charitable intent. The worthless papers and the fund for their expansion and publication constituted a mistaken choice of method which could accomplish nothing. The notes, where rational, were intended to be philosophical in nature; therefore the way to give effect to the charitable intent was to entrust the fund to a reputable university department of philosophy.

OTHER PROBLEMS

The cases involving colleges and universities during the period 1946–50 encompass an amazing variety and range of facts and of law. Many of them can not be mentioned even in a most cursory way at this point, for this entire volume is a terse condensation of the story. In its several chapters the careful reader will discern apparent trends other than the few which have been briefly discussed in the foregoing paragraphs. He will note that in Oklahoma at two state institutions a campus water system and heating and power plant have been financed by the "self-liquidating" method by virtue of charging a student fee for these services, and he may ponder the social implications of that fact. He will note a larger number of cases than usual concerned with the institutional real property of both private and public institutions. He will observe the fortunes of private colleges and of fraternity chapters under the impact of local zoning regulations. It is not necessary to carry the preview further. Each one of the approximately 190 decisions in some 40 jurisdictions carries its own intrinsic interest.

PART ONE

UNIVERSITY AND COLLEGE PERSONNEL

CHAPTER I

HIGHER EDUCATION AS A RIGHT

WHETHER education at the college level is a "necessary" which a parent owes his child is a question which has appeared and reappeared in American courts for more than a century. In recent years it arises occasionally in the adjudication of the obligations of divorced parents. In the nineteenth century some courts attempted to distinguish between vocational and general education, holding that the former could be a "necessary" in circumstances where the latter could not. It is, of course, impossible to draw a sharp boundary between the two types of education; and it appears probable that the effort to separate the two for purposes of determining what is a "necessary" may eventually be abandoned.

OBLIGATION OF DIVORCED PARENT

A considerable number of decisions in several states, beginning with the *Esteb Case* in the state of Washington in 1926, has gone a long way toward establishing the principle that a divorced father in modest or affluent financial circumstances may properly be ordered to contribute to the expenses at college of a son or daughter of college age. An Indiana appellate court rendered a contrary decision in a case where the father, under order to pay $40 a month for his daughter's support, petitioned for relief from the payments when she reached the age of eighteen and was graduated from high school in 1946. The adverse plea alleged that she wished to attend a university or college, and the trial court ordered the payments continued; but this judgment was reversed and remanded for a new trial. In so doing, the appellate court flatly declared: "It is settled in this state that a court has no authority to require a parent to provide funds to defray the expense of a general college education for a child," but left an apparent inference that a distinction might be made in favor of vocational or professional education.[1] This is an ultraconservative view.

A more liberal concept of what a daughter of college age may expect from a divorced parent was demonstrated in Tennessee. A prosperous business man, owning a lumber plant, furniture factory, and other real estate, was divorced in 1938, when his daughter was fourteen. Her custody was not awarded, but she chose to live with her mother. She attended and completed high school during the four years 1938–42, during which time her father gave her more than $2,000. Then, in the words of the court, "The father seems to have had the idea that he was no longer responsible for her maintenance after she reached her eighteenth birthday or that he need not send her to college." She attended Carson-Newman College from February 1942 to February 1944. During those two years she earned $144.72 by waiting on tables at the college, her father gave her $246.42, and her mother worked as a cook, laundress, and canning-factory operative to earn $737.49 which was spent to keep her in college. The mother then sued to compel the father to reimburse her for his appropriate share of the college expenses and won a judgment for $550, which was affirmed by a Tennessee court of appeals. The court had no doubt that the obligation to pay college expenses rested on the parents and declared that in Tennessee it rests upon both, equally and jointly; but a controversy between them as to the proper contribution of each is determinable only by equitable principles, with due regard to the condition and means of each.[2]

"EDUCATION" IS BROADER THAN "TUITION"

In New York a husband and wife executed a separation agreement under which the husband undertook to pay for the educa-

1 *Hachet* v. *Hachet* (Ind.), 71 N.E. 2d 927 (1947).
2 *Atchley* v. *Atchley* (Tenn. App.), 194 S.W. 2d 252 (1946).

tion of a daughter through her twenty-first year at a rate not to exceed $750 per year. Later he contended that his obligation was only for tuition fees, and not for board and lodging for his daughter while attending college away from home. Said Judge Coleman of the city court, "I cannot agree. 'Education' of a girl at college away from home must include board and lodging." [3]

[3] *Stern* v. *Kastor*, 186 Misc. 781, 60 N.Y.S. 2d 240 (1946).

CHAPTER II

STUDENTS: ADMISSION, SEGREGATION

THE issue which overshadowed all others between 1946 and 1950 was that of the admission of qualified Negro applicants to graduate and professional courses in state-supported universities and colleges in the states whose statutes require segregation of the races in educational institutions. Four new decisions of the Supreme Court of the United States, and other decisions of inferior federal courts and of state courts, have established several principles: (1) the right of access to equal facilities *within the borders of the state,* as enunciated by the late Chief Justice Charles Evans Hughes in the *Gaines Case* of 1938,[1] is a personal and present right, and delay in opening the facilities for persons of one race while holding them open for persons of another race can not be condoned; (2) a hastily established, makeshift, segregated graduate or professional school can not be said to be "substantially equivalent" to a long-established, reputable, and duly accredited graduate or professional school in a state university; and (3) having admitted a qualified Negro student to its state university, a state is further obligated to give him the same treatment as students of other races, and not handicap him by restricting his use of seats in classroom, library, or cafeteria, so as to cut off his opportunities to discuss his work with other students.

The litigated cases here mentioned have arisen in no fewer than six states—Kentucky, Louisiana, Maryland, Oklahoma, South Carolina, and Texas—and similar issues are understood

[1] *State of Missouri ex rel. Gaines* v. *Canada et al.*, 305 U.S. 337, 59 S. Ct. 232, 83 L. Ed. 207 (1938). Digested at pp. 5–6 in *The Colleges and the Courts, 1936–40.*

to be in preparation or on their way upward from the trial courts in some other states of the Southeast.

EQUAL FACILITIES FOR GRADUATE AND PROFESSIONAL EDUCATION: THE SIPUEL CASE

Nine years after the *Gaines Case* (1938) was decided, the Supreme Court of the United States again dealt with the issue in the form of Ada Lois Sipuel's suit in the courts of Oklahoma and of the United States to gain admission as a student in the law school of the University of Oklahoma. The Oklahoma supreme court conceded that the Constitution of the United States prohibits discrimination against persons of any race, but spoke with great fervor, if not too convincingly, of the law and custom of the state regarding racial segregation:

> This policy has been established and perpetuated . . . by voters and taxpayers and educators and patrons of both races, as if for the greater good of both races in Oklahoma. So that, without regard to distances, conveniences or desires, or any other consideration, a Negro child or pupil may not enter a white school nor a white child or pupil enter a Negro school.

Conceding, too, that the state must provide within its own borders substantially equal educational facilities for qualified citizens of all races, the court decided that Oklahoma was obligated to set up a segregated law school for such qualified Negro applicants as might request it, and concluded somewhat lamely that the state must be allowed ample time in which to accomplish this step, after demand for it had been made by prospective patrons of the school.[2]

The element of delay was the weak point in the armor of the state of Oklahoma when the case was appealed and argued on review before the Supreme Court of the United States late in 1947; and on January 12, 1948, a curt opinion of the high tribunal by Mr. Justice Wiley Rutledge declared:

[2] *Sipuel* v. *Board of Regents of The University of Oklahoma, et al.,* 199 Okla. 36, 180 P. 2d 135 (1947).

The petitioner is entitled to secure legal education afforded by a state institution. To this time, it has been denied her although during the same period many white applicants have been afforded legal education by the state. The state must provide it for her in conformity with the equal-protection clause of the Fourteenth Amendment and provide it as soon as it does for applicants of any other group.[3]

Five days later the supreme court of Oklahoma issued a writ directing the State Regents for Higher Education "to afford to plaintiff, and all others similarly situated, an opportunity to commence the study of law at a state institution as soon as citizens of other groups are afforded such opportunity," in conformity with the federal Constitution and with the Oklahoma constitutional and statutory provisions requiring segregation in schools.[4] On January 22 the district court of Cleveland County (where the University of Oklahoma is located) entered an order directing the regents, if a segregated law school for Negroes were ready to function "at the designated time applicants of any other group may hereafter apply for admission to the first-year class of the School of Law of the University of Oklahoma," then not to admit the plaintiff to the University of Oklahoma; but if a segregated law school were not ready, then either to enroll the plaintiff temporarily in the University of Oklahoma, only until the separate law school should be ready, or not to enroll any applicant of any group to the first-year class of the School of Law of the University of Oklahoma until the separate law school should be ready to function.

Miss Sipuel's attorneys then asked the Supreme Court of the United States for leave to file a petition for a writ of *mandamus* to compel compliance with that court's opinion of January 12. The motion was denied on February 16, 1948, in an opinion in which the majority of the justices decided that the order of the

[3] *Ada Lois Sipuel* v. *Board of Regents of The University of Oklahoma, et al.*, 332 U.S. 631, 68 S. Ct. 299, 92 L. Ed. 247 (1948).

[4] *Sipuel* v. *Board of Regents of University of Oklahoma* (Okla.), 190 P. 2d 437 (1948).

district court was in conformity with the mandate in the decision of January 12; and that questions as to whether the mandate was actually being executed must first be passed upon by the courts of Oklahoma before being heard in the United States Supreme Court. There were two dissents. Mr. Justice Frank Murphy recorded his belief that a hearing should have been had to determine whether the Oklahoma court orders were an evasion of the mandate of January 12; and Mr. Justice Wiley Rutledge wrote a separate opinion trenchantly declaring that the Oklahoma court orders did not follow the mandate, because, said he:

Obviously no separate law school could be established elsewhere overnight capable of giving petitioner a legal education equal to that afforded by the state's long-established and well-known state university law school. Nor could the necessary time be taken to create such facilities, while continuing to deny them to the petitioner, without incurring the delay which would continue the discrimination our mandate required to end at once.[5]

As we shall soon see, Mr. Justice Rutledge's cogent dissent was to be adopted by the whole court and become the law of the land a little less than two and a half years later.

THE MC LAURIN CASE

It was also in 1948 that G. W. McLaurin, a Negro teacher in Oklahoma, holding a master's degree, gained admission to the graduate school of the University of Oklahoma as a prospective candidate for the degree of Doctor of Philosophy. The three-judge federal court, after considering the fact that his application had been rejected solely on account of his race, decided as follows:

We hold, in conformity with the equal protection clause of the Fourteenth Amendment, that plaintiff is entitled to secure a post-graduate course of study in education leading to a doctor's degree in

[5] *Ada Lois Sipuel Fisher* v. *Justices of the Supreme Court of the State of Oklahoma, the Board of Regents of The University of Oklahoma, et al.,* 333 U.S. 147, 68 S. Ct. 389, 92 L. Ed. 604 (1948).

this state in a state institution, and that he is entitled to secure it as soon as it is afforded to any other applicant.

Insofar as any statute or law of the state of Oklahoma denies or deprives this plaintiff admission to the University of Oklahoma for the purpose of pursuing the course of study he seeks, . . . it is unconstitutional and unenforceable. . . . We simply hold that insofar as they [such statutes] are sought to be enforced in this particular case, they are inoperative.

"Assuming that the law having been declared, the State will comply," the court refrained from issuing injunctive relief, but retained jurisdiction of the case with power to issue necessary further orders and decrees.[6]

A year later McLaurin came again to the court, complaining that although he had been admitted to the university, he was nevertheless deprived of the equal protection of the law because he was required to sit in a designated seat apart from other students in his classes, study at a segregated table in the library, and eat in the cafeteria at a designated table and at a specified time so as to separate him as far as possible from other students. This time the court somewhat surprisingly declared that "The classification based upon racial distinctions is reasonable, founded in the public policy of the state, and does not operate to deprive the plaintiff of the equal protection of the laws."

This opinion was resoundingly reversed by the Supreme Court of the United States on June 5, 1950. Speaking of the discrimination just described, Mr. Chief Justice Fred M. Vinson said:

The result is that appellant is handicapped in his pursuit of effective graduate instruction. Such restrictions impair and inhibit his ability to study, to engage in discussions and exchange views with other students, and, in general, to learn his profession.

Our society grows increasingly complex, and our need for trained leaders increases correspondingly. Appellant's case represents, perhaps, the epitome of that need, for he is attempting to obtain an advanced degree in education, to become, by definition, a leader and

[6] *McLaurin* v. *Oklahoma State Regents for Higher Education et al.* (U.S.D.C.), 87 F. Supp. 526 (1948).

trainer of others. Those who will come under his guidance and influence must be directly affected by the education he receives. Their own education and development will necessarily suffer to the extent that his training is unequal to that of his classmates. State-imposed restrictions which produce such results cannot be sustained. . . .

Appellant, having been admitted to a state-supported graduate school, must receive the same treatment at the hands of the state as students of other races.[7]

THE SWEATT CASE

Parallel to the *Sipuel* and *McLaurin* cases in Oklahoma was the *Sweatt* case in Texas. Heman Marion Sweatt, a Negro fully qualified for admission to the law school of the University of Texas, was refused solely because of his race in 1946. In June of that year the trial court ruled that a writ of *mandamus* to compel his admission would be issued unless the state established substantially equal segregated law school facilities by December 17, 1946. A statute of 1945 had already changed the name of Prairie View State College (a Negro institution) to Prairie View State University and authorized it to establish schools of law, medicine, and engineering "whenever there is any demand for same." The legislature of 1947, however, ignored that policy and created the Texas State University for Negroes (located at Houston), appropriating $2,000,000 for capital outlay and $500,000 for operating expenses for the biennium ending August 31, 1949. This new institution was authorized to provide "all courses of higher learning . . . in order that the separate state universities for Negroes shall at all times offer equal educational opportunities and training as that available to other persons of this state."

Moreover, that session of the legislature directed the Board of Regents of the University of Texas, in the interim, to establish forthwith upon demand, a law school to be known as the "School of Law of the Texas State University for Negroes,"

[7] *McLaurin v. Oklahoma State Regents for Higher Education et al.*, 339 U.S. 637, 70 S. Ct. 851, 94 L. Ed. 1149 (1950), reversing *Same* (U.S.D.C.), 87 F. Supp. 528 (1949).

and to be subsequently transferred to the Board of Directors of the Texas State University for Negroes. An appropriation of $100,000 was made for the "interim" law school, and the Regents proceeded to establish it in Austin in a building near the University of Texas and accessible to the Supreme Court Library, which was to be available to Negro law students. The teaching was to be done by regular professors in the law school of the University of Texas. Sweatt refused to enroll in this "interim" law school; and his case having been carried up to a court of civil appeals, his petition for a writ of *mandamus* to compel the law school of the University of Texas to admit him was denied by that court in 1948. *Certiorari* was granted by the United States Supreme Court in 1949, and it transpired that the *McLaurin* case from Oklahoma and the *Sweatt* case from Texas were argued together before the high tribunal, and decided together in decisions announced June 5, 1950.

In the *Sweatt* case, reversing the decision of the Texas court of civil appeals, Mr. Chief Justice Fred M. Vinson, after discussing both the "interim" law school and the permanent law school projected at the Texas State University for Negroes, said for the court:

Whether the University of Texas Law School is compared with the original or the new law school for Negroes, we cannot find substantial equality in the educational opportunities offered white and Negro law students by the State. In terms of number of the faculty, variety of courses and opportunity for specialization, size of the student body, scope of the library, availability of law review and similar activities, the University of Texas Law School is superior. What is more important, the University of Texas Law School possesses to a far greater degree those qualities which are incapable of objective measurement but which make for greatness in a law school. Such qualities, to name but a few, include reputation of the faculty, experience of the administration, position and influence of the alumni, standing in the community, traditions and prestige. It is difficult to believe that one who had a free choice between these law schools would consider the question close.

Moreover, although the law is a highly learned profession, we are well aware that it is an intensely practical one. The law school, the proving ground for legal learning and practice cannot be effective in isolation from the individuals and institutions with which the law interacts. Few students and no one who has practiced law would choose to study in an academic vacuum, removed from the interplay of ideas and the exchange of views with which the law is concerned. The law school to which Texas is willing to admit petitioner excludes from its student body members of the racial groups which number 85% of the population of the State and include most of the lawyers, witnesses, jurors, judges, and other officials with whom petitioner will inevitably be dealing when he becomes a member of the Texas Bar. With such a substantial and significant segment of society excluded, we cannot conclude that the education offered petitioner is substantially equal to that which he would receive if admitted to the University of Texas Law School. . . .

We hold that the Equal Protection Clause of the Fourteenth Amendment requires that petitioner be admitted to the University of Texas Law School.[8]

RECENT DECISIONS IN LOWER FEDERAL COURTS

Forerunners of the foregoing decisions of the nation's highest tribunal may be found in inferior federal courts. For example, in 1947 such a court, adjudicating the rights of qualified Negro applicants for law school facilities in South Carolina, did not go much beyond the principle announced in the *Gaines Case* of 1938, but sought to implement it. District Judge Waring concluded the opinion of the court as follows:

The order of this court will provide that the State furnish to the plaintiff and others in like plight law school facilities equal to those at the University of South Carolina, either at the university itself, or State College, or any other satisfactory institution in the State, or furnish none to anyone; and furthermore, I think it only fair and just, in view of all the circumstances, that the State of South Carolina be granted until the next law school semester which will open in the month of September 1947.[9]

[8] *Sweatt* v. *Painter et al.*, 339 U.S. 629, 70 S. Ct. 848, 94 L. Ed. 1115 (1950), reversing and remanding *Same* (Tex. Civ. App.), 210 S.W. 2d 442 (1948).

[9] *Wrighten* v. *Board of Trustees of University of South Carolina* (U.S.D.C.), 72 F. Supp. 948 (1947).

Another federal court in Kentucky went further in 1949. Here a qualified Negro wished to pursue a Ph.D. degree in history. The University of Kentucky, rejecting him because of his race and color, defended on the ground that it had entered into a contract whereby a graduate school for Negroes was proposed to be operated at the Kentucky State College for Negroes at Frankfort, with the faculty commuting from the University at Lexington, and the students being transported to the library of the University at Lexington. This, said the court in the words of Chief Judge Ford, "would be entirely insufficient and inadequate" to provide substantially equal facilities, and emphasized the fact that the Negro graduate students at Frankfort would be denied the advantage of seminars under resident instructors, would not have convenient library facilities for graduate study, and "would be subject to the disadvantage of being taught by a migratory faculty whose duties and responsibilities in respect to the proposed graduate school would necessarily be secondary and subordinate to their duties and responsibilities to the University." Thus the court issued a declaratory judgment to the effect that qualified Negro applicants are entitled to be admitted to the graduate and professional schools of the University of Kentucky until the Commonwealth shall provide substantially equal facilities at a separate institution within its borders.[10]

A 1950 case in a Louisiana federal court went a step further, both as to substantive law and procedural remedy. The state university refused Negroes admission to its department of law, and the state undertook in 1947 to establish at Southern University (a state institution for Negroes) "a *bona fide* law school for Negroes of the highest possible standards." The court readily concluded that this policy "has not in this comparatively short period of time been effectuated," and held that the law school at Southern University was not substantially

[10] *Johnson* v. *Board of Trustees of University of Kentucky et al.* (U.S.D.C.), 83 F. Supp. 707 (1949).

equal to the department of law at the state university. Here the remedy was the issuance of an interlocutory injunction, under Section 2281 of the Federal Judicial Code, restraining the enforcement of the order of the governing board of the state university which denied the plaintiff admission.[11] The United States Supreme Court granted review of the case, and affirmed the judgment by *per curiam* order on January 2, 1951.[12]

CASES IN STATE COURTS

A Texas case is of interest only as a bypath. A Negro wishing a refresher course in dentistry sued for *mandamus* to compel the Regents of the University of Texas to establish at Austin a branch university for colored youth. A section of the Texas Constitution provides that the legislature shall, when practicable, establish such an institution, "to be located by a vote of the people"; and an election for the purpose in 1882 resulted in the selection of Austin; but the section is not self-executing, and it is not a mandate to the Board of Regents. Thus the suit failed.[13]

Of more importance is the 1950 Maryland decision ordering the University of Maryland to act upon an application for admission to its nursing school, which had been denied solely because the applicant was a Negro girl. This case is of especial interest because, under a regional compact enacted as Chapter 282, *Maryland Acts* of 1949, and constituting a contract between the state of Maryland and the Board of Control for Southern Regional Education, the plaintiff Negro girl was offered a course in nursing at Meharry Medical College at Nashville, Tennessee (an institution for Negroes) at a total cost to her, including living and traveling expenses, not exceeding the total costs she would have incurred as a student at the University of

[11] *Board of Supervisors of Louisiana State University and Agricultural and Mechanical College et al.* v. *Wilson* (U.S.D.C.); opinion filed Oct. 7, 1950.

[12] *Same*, affirmed by U.S. Supreme Court (No. 436); reported in 19 *U.S. Law Week* 3183, January 2, 1951.

[13] *Givens et al.* v. *Woodward et al.* (Tex. Civ. App.), 207 S.W. 2d 234; error denied (Tex.), 208 S.W. 2d 363 (1948).

Maryland school of nursing. This she declined. There was detailed and uncontradicted testimony that the Meharry nursing school is superior to the nursing school at the University of Maryland; but this, held the court, is immaterial. Under the *Gaines* and *Sipuel* decisions, the plaintiff is entitled to equal facilities within the borders of her home state, and may reject an offer of equal or superior facilities outside those borders.

In discussing the case, the court assumed but did not decide, that the regional compact administered by the Board of Control for Southern Regional Education is constitutional and valid, though made without the consent of Congress. There is question as to whether the Constitution of the United States actually makes the consent of Congress requisite to the validity of such compacts.[14] The United States Supreme Court denied *certiorari* on October 9, 1950.

SEGREGATION IN ST. LOUIS TEACHERS COLLEGES SUSTAINED

In large cities in the "border states" where racial segregation in schools prevails, the maintenance of two segregated local teachers colleges is subject to attack as a relatively costly and educationally inefficient arrangement. Moreover, there are undoubtedly instances wherein the facilities for the education of Negro teachers are in fact not substantially equivalent to those for white teachers. It is only this latter issue that can be considered in the courts. Questions of the economy and efficiency of the scheme of teacher-education as a whole, whether segregated or non-segregated, are not for the courts, but for the legislative authorities. The courts may examine, however, the quality of the facilities and work of white and Negro institutions in the same community, for the purpose of comparing them to determine the question of whether or not they are substantially equivalent.

In St. Louis, Marjorie V. Toliver, a Negro girl aged 20 who

[14] *McCready* v. *Byrd et al.* (Md.), 73 A. 2d 8 (1950); *Byrd et al.* v. *McCready*, *certiorari* denied, 340 U.S. 827, by U.S. Supreme Court (No. 219); reported in 19 *U.S. Law Week* 3097, Oct. 9, 1950.

had completed two semesters in Stowe Teachers College (for Negroes) sought a writ of *mandamus* to compel her admission forthwith to Harris Teachers College (white), alleging that the facilities available to her at Stowe were not substantially equivalent to those available to white students at Harris. The trial court issued a peremptory writ, but the judgment was reversed and remanded by the supreme court of Missouri, which unanimously adopted the opinion of three commissioners assigned to the case. Considerable data relative to the faculties, physical plants, curricula, libraries, and laboratories of the two institutions were adduced in the opinion. At the time of the trial both were accredited by the American Association of Teachers Colleges and by the North Central Association of Colleges and Secondary Schools.

Stowe had a newer and more suitable physical plant and location than Harris, and a higher teacher-student ratio. Annual expenditures per student were nearly identical for the two institutions. The opinion concluded:

> In the instant case the constituted authorities are endeavoring to discharge their mandatory duty of providing substantially equal facilities to the segregated groups within their territorial jurisdiction. . . . The main differences of record appear to exist in some of the laboratory facilities, differences considered not to constitute substantial inequality. There is no affirmation showing the plaintiff is adversely affected by these differences.[15]

IS THERE A RIGHT OF ADMISSION TO A PRIVATELY CONTROLLED INSTITUTION?

Traditionally the privately controlled universities and colleges have been regarded as having a right to exercise complete control over their own admission policies, unless limited in that respect by the terms of their charters. There has always been a differing school of thought, however, in which they are looked upon as performing an important public function at the

[15] *State ex rel. Toliver* v. *Board of Education of City of St. Louis et al.* (Mo.), 230 S.W. 2d 724 (1950).

sufferance of the state, and, therefore, as a species of remote deputies of the state and more or less subject to the same constitutional limitations as the state's own direct agencies.

Northwestern University reserves the right to reject any applicant for admission for any reason which it considers adequate, and its authority to maintain such a rule has apparently been vindicated in protracted litigation.

A precocious boy born near the end of 1929 applied for admission to the liberal arts college of the university in September 1944 and took and passed the entrance examinations, but his application was rejected on the ground that he was too young, being then only 14 years of age. He enrolled in the university's evening school of commerce in 1944–45 and successfully completed fourteen credit hours of work. In June 1945 he was denied admission to the summer course in commerce, and in September he was denied admission to the college of liberal arts, both refusals being because he had in the meantime instituted a suit to compel the university to admit him. This suit was dismissed by the local superior court, and an appeal was taken direct to the supreme court of Illinois on the ground that the plaintiff's constitutional rights were involved. The supreme court ruled that there was no constitutional question concerned and accordingly transferred the appeal to the intermediate appellate court, where the record was reviewed and a judgment unfavorable to the plaintiff was rendered.

It was the opinion of the court that the university had protected its position fully by stating in its catalogs of 1943–45 that it was not possible to admit all applicants who passed the entrance examinations, and by placing in the catalog for 1945–46 a statement that the university reserved the right to exclude any applicant for any reason deemed sufficient by it.

Said Judge Kiley:

> Under its charter the university had the power to adopt whatever rules it deemed necessary to the proper attainment of the university purpose. . . . The only compulsion arising out of the university's

charter with respect to admissions is that "no particular religious faith shall be required of those who become students." There is no point before us based on breach of this command.

A line must be drawn somewhere if there are more qualified students than can be accommodated. The educational facilities of this country have been strained to the utmost by the great number of postwar students. It is a matter of common knowledge that thousands have been turned away from most, if not all, of the colleges and universities in the United States.[16]

In 1948 the United States Supreme Court denied a writ of *certiorari* in this case. The outcome, no doubt, will be regarded as a strengthening of the ramparts defending the right of a privately controlled educational institution to select its own students, free from state compulsion. The way is open for the state to provide facilities for higher education for all qualified applicants at its own state universities and colleges.

[16] *People ex rel. Tinkoff et al.* v. *Northwestern University et al.*, 396 Ill. 233, 71 N.E. 2d 156 (1947); appeal transferred, 333 Ill. App. 224, 77 N.E. 2d 345 (1947). *Certiorari* denied, 335 U.S. 829, 69 S. Ct. 37, 93 L. Ed. 383 (1948).

CHAPTER III

STUDENTS: VOTING RESIDENCE, INDEMNIFICATION FOR PERSONAL INJURIES, OTHER MATTERS

THIS chapter covers not only the subjects specifically mentioned in its title, but also a heterogeneous collection of other cases involving students. Some of these latter are not concerned directly with the relationships between the student and the institution he attends, but are nevertheless of passing interest.

VOTING RESIDENCE

For many decades the courts generally held that one who came to a college town solely for the purpose of attending college there, and with a presumptive intent to depart upon completion of his college course, acquired no domicile there such as to entitle him to vote in the college town in popular elections. It was often difficult to establish exceptions to this rule, or to obtain modifications of it, even in the cases of students who were wholly self-supporting and who avowed an intent to make the college town their permanent dwelling place. The late 1940s, bringing to almost every campus an influx of war-veteran students of whom many were married and brought with them their wives and young children, seem to have worked something of a revolution in that respect.

Thus when Columbia University established "Shanks Village" (a part of the military reservation known as Camp Shanks) in Rockland County, New York, by leasing the housing from the Federal Public Housing Administration to be rented only to student veterans who had families, a protracted controversy ensued over the right to vote in the local election district. The trial court and the appellate division readily decided that the wives and parents of students, living with them in "Shanks Village," must be allowed to vote in the local election district; but adhered to the ancient rule that the *students* themselves were not so entitled. The New York Court of Appeals reversed this latter part of the decision, and said tersely:

> These students are family men, not college boys away from their parental homes. True, their tenure of occupancy at Shanks Village can continue only while they are students, but, since they have no other homes, their tenure is "temporary" or "indefinite" only in the same sense as the tenure of the occupant of a city apartment house.
>
> These petitioners have shown their eligibility to vote from the only residences they have. As to the right to vote of the wives or parents of veteran-students, we cannot see that there is any doubt whatever.[1]

The supreme court of Arkansas was somewhat more conservative in a 1949 case in which the primary election for the Democratic nomination for municipal judge was won by a vote of 975 to 910, and it was alleged that 170 student-veterans at the University of Arkansas had voted, most of them for the winner. The trial court announced the rule that "a student who comes to Fayetteville for the sole purpose of securing an education does so without making a change of residence. It is necessary to have a *bona fide* intention to make Fayetteville his home permanently or for an indefinite period and not to limit it to the time necessary to get an education." The court then proceeded to examine individually the students who had voted, and found some qualified and others disqualified. When the state supreme court reviewed the case it approved the rule announced, and declared:

[1] *Robbins et al.* v. *Chamberlain et al.*, 297 N.Y. 108, 75 N.E. 2d 617 (1947), modifying and affirming *Same*, 272 App. Div. 1034, 74 N.Y.S. 2d 830 (1947), which had affirmed *Same*, 189 Misc. 1020.

A large number of young students had served in the Army and upon their discharge had entered the University under the G.I. Bill of Rights. This fact did not render them residents within the meaning of our election laws, and the court so properly held.

The supreme court also approved the test of eligibility

which is to the effect that a person removing from his old home did not acquire a new domicile until he had abandoned his old one. In other words, for the purpose of voting a person does not have two domiciles with a right to choose between them. His domicile is either at one place or the other.

Thus the Arkansas supreme court hewed close to the line of established precedents. The decision of the trial court was approved as to the *ratio decidendi* or crucial issue, but reversed and remanded merely for the correction of certain procedural errors which might change the result.[2]

It may be noted that change in the concept of the voting residence of students will probably be accelerated by the modern mobility of population, as indicated in the New York decision. There is some significance in the fact that in the United States Census of 1950, for the first time in history noncommuting college students were enumerated for census purposes as residents of the college town. There, indeed, is the place where they normally spend three fourths or more of their time for periods ranging up to four or more years.

INDEMNIFICATION FOR PERSONAL INJURIES

There is a widespread custom of paying, out of the funds collected as gate receipts, the medical expenses of college football players who sustain physical injuries as a result of playing the game. Can this be lawfully done at a state institution where a statute requires such funds to be deposited in a State Special Athletic Receipts Fund, and authorizes the money to be used "to defray the cost of maintaining the athletic department and the athletic program" at the institution? The supreme court of West

[2] *Ptak* v. *Jameson* (Ark.), 220 S.W. 2d 592 (1949).

Virginia answers yes, holding that medical expenses of injured players, in view of the custom at West Virginia University and elsewhere, are expenses incidental to maintaining the athletic program; and payment thereof does not conflict with the section of the state constitution which forbids the state to "become responsible for the debts of any county, city, township, corporation, or person." The court then proceeded to allay the qualms of the state auditor by ordering him to requisition $256.35 to pay medical expenses incurred by one J. Robert Murphy, a university football player who was injured in a game.[3]

A very different question was presented when persons injured by the collapse of a metal grandstand while spectators at an athletic contest at Purdue University proceeded against the manufacturer and seller of the grandstand in a tort action, alleging that the grandstand was defective and that the manufacturer's negligence was the proximate cause of their injuries. Under precedents long followed in most jurisdictions, no recovery would be possible because there was plainly no "privity of contract" between the manufacturer and the injured persons. A federal district court, however, declared that this old rule has been "swallowed up by exceptions." Refusing to accept it as a basis for the defendant's motion to dismiss the case, the court continued:

> If the nature of a thing is reasonably certain to place life or limb in peril when negligently made, it is then a thing of danger to those who it is contemplated will use it, irrespective of privity between such users and defendants. In other words the inquiry is simply whether the injury charged is the natural and probable consequence of the wrong, such a consequence as might or ought to have been foreseen as likely to flow from the wrong.[4]

Additional cases involving the indemnification of students for personal injuries are treated *infra* in Chapter XVIII.

[3] *State ex rel. Board of Governors of West Virginia University* v. *Sims* (W. Va.), 59 S.E. 2d 705 (1950).

[4] *McCloud* v. *Leavitt Corporation et al.* (U.S.D.C.), 79 F. Supp. 286 (1948).

DEDUCTION, FOR FEDERAL INCOME TAX PURPOSES, OF UNIVERSITY SUMMER SCHOOL EXPENSES OF A PUBLIC SCHOOL TEACHER

Nora Payne Hill, a Virginia schoolteacher of 27 years' standing, in 1945 found that her certificate was about to expire and could not be renewed unless she obtained additional college credits or passed an examination covering five books on the list of the Virginia Teachers' Reading Circle. She elected to attend the Columbia University summer school, and did so at an outlay of $239.50 for expenses. This she deducted in computing her net taxable income for the calendar year. Both the Commissioner of Internal Revenue and the United States Tax Court disallowed the deduction, but this decision was at length reversed by the United States Circuit Court of Appeals. The conclusions of the court, in an opinion by Circuit Judge Dobie, were that in this case the summer school expenses were not personal in nature, but were ordinary and necessary in carrying on the defendant's "trade or business." Judge Dobie pointed out that in other cases movie actors were allowed to deduct expenses to maintain physical fitness, and opera singers were permitted to deduct money paid to a voice coach. There was also a ruling in force, said he, to the effect that the

> dues paid by teachers to professional societies, the price of their subscriptions for educational journals connected with their profession, and the expenses of traveling and meals and lodging incurred in attending teachers' conventions in this country, if they are not reimbursed for such expenses, are . . . deductible. . . .

He made it clear, however, that the decision in this case was based on the particular facts, especially that Virginia law required the teacher to obtain additional education in order to continue the practice of her profession; and the opinion expressly refrained from declaring void a ruling of 1921 which stipulates that "The expenses incurred by schoolteachers in attending summer-school are in the nature of personal expenses incurred in advancing their education and are not deductible in computing net income."[5] This decision does not abrogate that rule, but only opens an exception for teachers who are under legal compulsion to obtain further education or lose their professional licenses.

IS STUDENT LIABLE TO AVIATION SCHOOL FOR ACCIDENTAL DAMAGE TO AIRPLANE?

At a private airport and flying school in South Dakota a student took the prescribed instruction and obtained a private pilot's license. Later he began further instruction leading to a commercial pilot's license, and while doing "elementary lights or pylons" he lost altitude and crashed the plane owned by the school. The school sued for damages, alleging that the crash was due to the student's negligence as a matter of law. The supreme court of South Dakota affirmed a trial court judgment for the defendant, based on a jury verdict in his favor. Conceding that in such cases it is often difficult to distinguish between negligence and lack of skill, the court maintained that it is not a question of law, but a question of fact for the jury; and that any damage resulting from a student's lack of skill is one of the risks a flying school assumes in its training program. The school is chargeable with knowledge of its student's degree of skill.[6]

ENFORCEMENT OF RULE PROHIBITING LIQUOR-SELLING NEAR CAMPUS

The proprietor of a retail liquor store in Nashville, located 400 to 500 feet from the edge of the campus of Fisk University, and 700 feet from the entrance thereof, sought a writ of *mandamus* to compel the State Commissioner of Finance and Taxation to issue him a license. A Nashville city ordinance forbade such an establishment "within 600 feet of a school or college campus," and an existing rule of the State Commissioner for-

[5] *Hill* v. *Commissioner of Internal Revenue* (U.S.C.C.A.), 181 F. 2d 906 (1950).
[6] *Vee Bar Airport* v. *De Vries* (S. Dak.), 43 N.W. 2d 369 (1950).

bade licensing when "in too close proximity to a church, school, or other public institution, or otherwise inimical to the public interest." Sustaining the enforcement of the Commissioner's rule in this case, the Tennessee supreme court declared, in the words of Special Justice Tomlinson: "The regulation . . . is very clearly in the interest of the health, safety and morals of the young men and women attending our colleges." [7]

TICKET-SCALPING, EXCEPT BY LICENSEES, A STATUTORY OFFENSE IN TEXAS

A Texas statute of 1941 stipulates that any person selling tickets to a sports event at a price greater than that printed thereon shall first obtain a license from the Comptroller of Public Accounts, and provides penalties for violation prior to the football game between the University of Texas and Southern Methodist University, to be played November 1, 1947, an individual was arrested and convicted of offering two $3 tickets at a price of $15 each. Assessment of a fine of $100 and a penalty of 45 days in jail was affirmed.[8]

STREET SPEECH BY STUDENT AS DISORDERLY CONDUCT

On March 8, 1949, a meeting to be addressed on the subject of racial discrimination and civil liberties by O. John Rogge, a former Assistant Attorney General of the United States, was scheduled in the Syracuse Hotel at Syracuse, New York. The meeting was under the auspices of an organization known as the Young Progressives. At about 6:30 P.M. a Syracuse University student was addressing an open-air assembly at a street corner, urging his hearers to attend the scheduled meeting in the evening. He spoke in a loud, high-pitched voice, through an amplifier on an automobile parked adjacent to the box on which he stood. In the course of his remarks he spoke of Mayor Costello of Syracuse as a "champagne-sipping bum," said President

[7] *State ex rel. Brown* v. *McCanless* (Tenn.), 195 S.W. 2d 619 (1946).
[8] *Humphrey* v. *State* (Tex. Cr. App.), 212 S.W. 2d 159 (1948).

Truman was a bum, and referred to the American Legion as "Nazi Gestapo agents." He appealed to the colored people in particular, and said Negroes did not have equal rights and that they should rise up in arms and fight for them.

Two police officers came upon the scene as the result of a telephoned report, and found a somewhat restless, muttering crowd. One man approached the officers and said, "If you don't get that son-of-a-bitch off, I will go over and get him off there myself." Others made similar remarks, and the officers then intervened, not to arrest the student, but to persuade him to dismiss the assembly. After he refused three successive requests to get down off his box, one of the officers placed him under arrest. He was charged and convicted of disorderly conduct under Section 722 of the New York Penal Law. The conviction was affirmed by the Court of Appeals, in an opinion in which Judge Conway said:

> Where both the audience and the speaker are inevitably proceeding toward an eruption of civil strife—where, indeed, both seem to be working up to a pitch where serious disorder might well be expected—the power and duty of the State to punish the speaker who refuses to desist after appropriate warning is clear.[9]

He also quoted Mr. Justice Owen J. Roberts in the classic 1940 case of *Cantwell* v. *Connecticut:*

> When clear and present danger of riot, disorder, interference with traffic on the public streets, or other immediate threat to public safety, peace, or order, appears, the power of the state to prevent or punish is obvious.

The Syracuse case went to the United States Supreme Court, on *certiorari,* and was affirmed by that tribunal early in 1951, with three of the justices dissenting.

The opinion of the majority was written by Mr. Chief Justice Vinson, who said:

> We are well aware that the ordinary murmurings and objections of a hostile audience cannot be allowed to silence a speaker, and are

[9] *People* v. *Feiner,* 300 N.Y. 391, 91 N.E. 2d 316 (1950).

also mindful of the possible danger of giving overzealous police officials complete discretion to break up otherwise lawful public meetings. . . . But we are not faced here with such a situation. It is one thing to say that the police cannot be used as an instrument for the oppression of unpopular views, and another to say that, when as here the speaker passes the bounds of argument or persuasion and undertakes incitement to riot, they are powerless to prevent a breach of the peace.[10]

Mr. Justice Douglas entered a dissent, with which Mr. Justice Minton concurred. Said they: "Police censorship has all the vices of the censorship from city halls which we have repeatedly struck down." Mr. Justice Black entered a separate dissent, in which he said: "The police of course have power to prevent breaches of the peace. But if, in the name of preserving order, they ever can interfere with a lawful public speaker, they first must make all reasonable efforts to protect him."

[10] *Irving Feiner* v. *People of the State of New York,* U.S. Supreme Court, No. 93, October Term, 1950 (January 15, 1951).

CHAPTER IV

TESTAMENTARY TRUSTS FOR STUDENT AID

IT is not strange that many philanthropically inclined persons, observing that poverty often prevents the most brilliant and promising students from attending a university or from obtaining maximum benefit from higher education, decide to create charitable trusts for the aid of such students. Scarcely any charitable purpose is more commonly espoused.

The principles of equity jurisprudence applicable to trusts of this kind are no different from those governing charitable trusts in general; but cases involving student aid are here treated in a brief chapter placed adjacent to other chapters concerned with student personnel. For a broader glimpse of educational trusts, reference may be made to the later chapters on the creation and operation of charitable trusts for higher education.

THE DEFINITION OF CHARITY IS NOT NARROW

A Texas testatrix established the G. Bedell Memorial Fund, a perpetual trust, directing that the income be used for several definitely designated charitable purposes, including gifts to a Protestant orphanage, a Y.M.C.A., a Y.W.C.A., and the American National Red Cross; and for scholarship loans "for worthy boys and girls," with each recipient to receive not more than $500 per year, and to obligate himself to repay the sum in full without interest as soon as able.

An heir to whom a building was devised for life, with the trust as remainderman, contested the will and claimed title in fee simple to the building in question, contending that the trust was invalid. Nothing is a charitable purpose, he argued, except an undertaking which might be conducted by government, and supported by taxation; and the presence of the words "benevolent" and "philanthropic" in the language of the will precludes a wholly charitable purpose, for these words may be construed as embracing private uses. The court readily struck down both of these untenable contentions, and declared the will created a valid charitable trust.[1]

CERTAINTY AND DEFINITENESS OF PURPOSE

The residuary estate of a Kansan was left in trust to three named persons, with power to sell or lease the real property and create a fund to aid "deserving men students graduating from the Pratt Junior College," by either gifts or loans, to complete their education at some university approved by the trustees. The trustees were also empowered to select their own successors by cooption.

When the will was contested, the principal attack was upon the word "deserving" as being too uncertain and indefinite to form a part of the basis of a valid charitable trust. Noting that the words of the will included several phrases unmistakably indicating a general charitable intent on the part of the testatrix, the Kansas supreme court correctly concluded that this is the essential element, sustaining the trust.[2]

The modern theory is that when the trust instrument makes manifest a general charitable intent, it need not specify details of the administration of the trust or set up elaborate or explicit plans for selection of beneficiaries.

Testamentary trusts for student aid were unsuccessfully attacked on the ground of indefiniteness and uncertainty in Colorado and Florida. Thus, a bequest to the trustees of the Methodist Episcopal Church, to be placed in a special trust

[1] *Moore* v. *Sellers* (Tex. Civ. App.), 201 S.W. 2d 248 (1947).

[2] *In re Porter's Estate: Harkrader* v. *Johnson*, 164 Kan. 92, 187 P. 2d 520 (1947).

fund, the income of which was to be used for the education of worthy, needy young Methodist men students of theology or medicine, created a valid charitable trust, as did also a parallel bequest in the same will to the Board of Christian Education of the Presbyterian Church in the United States of America in the same manner and for similar purposes.[3] Likewise valid was a trust created by a bequest to the executor of an estate, empowering him to use it "for the education and advancement of the learning of deserving young men or young women," and leaving him full discretion to fix the number and select the persons who would benefit from the trust, and to exhaust the entire fund for this purpose as he saw fit.[4]

TRUSTEES MAY ASK FOR JUDICIAL INSTRUCTIONS

A Delaware testatrix, forty years principal of Howard High School in Wilmington, died in 1930 leaving a will and codicil directing that her house should go to two named women as life tenants and, upon the death of the last survivor, should be sold and the proceeds deposited in trust with a local savings bank to provide a college or university scholarship for some worthy graduate of Howard High School to be selected by the faculty.

The first life tenant died in 1943, and soon thereafter the other became incapacitated, whereupon the court appointed an individual trustee to manage the estate.

This trustee entered a petition for instructions, her principal questions and the court's answers thereto being as follows: Would it be permissible to sell the property immediately and pay the income of the proceeds to the surviving life tenant? Yes. Public sale was directed. In view of the fact that the savings bank now limits individual deposits to only $250 per month, how should the proceeds be invested? In any manner conforming to the Delaware statute of 1935 relating to the investment

[3] *Galiger* v. *Armstrong* (Colo.), 165 P. 2d 1019 (1946).
[4] *Miller et al.* v. *Flowers* (Fla.), 27 So. 2d 667 (1946).

of trust funds. When the charitable use begins after the death of the life tenant, how shall the faculty select the beneficiary? Shall the scholarship be tenable for one year only or for longer periods? Let the faculty select by majority vote of the full-time teachers, as was its custom in determining policy matters in the day of the testatrix. Let the faculty likewise determine for what periods the scholarship shall be tenable.[5]

In Massachusetts a Roman Catholic priest who died in 1929 created certain testamentary trusts, one of which, with a corpus of about $15,000, was to provide annually in May a prize to the student in one of the Catholic colleges of New England who presented the best self-composed essay or other similar literary composition. The donor named a committee of three persons, including the Grand Knight of the Knights of Columbus, to arrange the annual contests; and directed that the contests were to be rotated annually among several named New England cities. There were other complicated features in the prescribed plan, and it transpired that for twenty years no contests were held. When the trustee then petitioned for instructions, the Massachusetts supreme judicial court concluded that the sole difficulty was the complexity of the directive provisions of the will, and that a simple plan would be possible. Therefore the case was remanded to the probate court with direction to set up a scheme for the administration of the trust. Brushing aside a contention that the trust should be held to have failed, and the fund returned to the estate, the court declared this to be an appropriate case for the application of the doctrine of *cy pres,* and stated an apt maxim: "Equity will presume that the donor would attach so much more importance to the object of the gift than to the mechanism by which he intended to accomplish it that he would prefer to alter the mechanism to the extent necessary to save the object."[6]

[5] *Woodlen* v. *Brodnax* (Del. Ch.), 57 A. 2d 752 (1948).

[6] *Worcester County Trust Company* v. *Grand Knight of Knights of Columbus* (Mass.), 92 N.E. 2d 579 (1950).

DEATH OF THE SOLE TRUSTEE DOES NOT INVALIDATE A CHARITABLE TRUST

As against the attack of heirs of the donor, a federal District Court sustained in 1950 a charitable testamentary trust in which a testatrix in Forth Worth, Texas, directed that all the income be used by the trustee to provide scholarships for worthy boys unable to pay their own expenses in Texas Christian University. The sole trustee, a natural person named in the will, died soon after the death of the testatrix, and it was argued unsuccessfully that this part of the will had not created a charitable trust, but only a personal agency which would terminate with the death of the agent. The charitable intent being clear and unmistakable, the court held that a valid charitable trust had been created.[7] It follows that the trust must be executed by a suitable trustee appointed by the appropriate court of equity.

THE DONOR HAS WIDE LATITUDE WITHIN WHICH TO PRESCRIBE A PLAN

A California testator bequeathed a substantial residuary estate to a bank in trust, with instructions to pay out of the income annually scholarships not exceeding $200 each for tuition at colleges and universities chosen by the recipients and approved by the trustees. It appeared that the income was sufficient to provide for about nine beneficiaries annually.

The trustee bank was directed to conduct each year a golf tournament on links selected by it in San Diego County, and all applicants for scholarships must be present and compete therein, though not necessarily residents of the county or of California. Applicants turning in scores higher than a specified "cutting score" were to be for that reason disqualified as ineligible for scholarships, and from among the remaining eligi-

[7] *Harrold* v. *First National Bank of Fort Worth et al.* (U.S.D.C.), 93 F. Supp. 882 (1950).

bles those having the lowest scores were to receive the awards.

The state tax authorities assessed a state inheritance tax against this part of the decedent's estate, questioning whether the gift was charitable and also contending that it was not exempt, even if charitable, under the terms of the tax act relating to domestic and foreign charities. The lower courts held that the eccentricity of the prescribed method of choosing the beneficiaries did not destroy the charitable character of the trust, and that no inheritance tax was collectible because the fact that the trust would be administered within the state would satisfy the statute.

Without disturbing the finding that the trust was a valid charitable one, the state supreme court reversed the judgment as to the inheritance tax, pointing out that under the exemption clause of 1917 the gift must be either to a charitable corporation within the state or limited to use within the state; and here neither condition was met.[8]

NEITHER INDIGENCE NOR SCHOLASTIC EXCELLENCE NEED BE REQUIRED OF BENEFICIARIES

Under a legacy to Cornell University for the establishment of the Nellie M. Lewis Scholarship in the College of Arts and Sciences, the income of the fund is to be awarded annually by the Scholarship Committee of the Federation of Cornell Women's Clubs to a woman undergraduate in any class. It may be re-awarded to the same holder, but it is not to be divided among more than one recipient. Attacking the validity of the trust, it was argued that the instrument does not require the beneficiaries to use the money for education, and might therefore result merely in the enrichment of individuals, without advancing education. Nor does it require that the beneficiaries demonstrate either financial need or superior scholastic records. These contentions did not trouble the New York surrogate. A gift to a university with the income thereof to students is ob-

[8] *In re Fleming's Estate: Kuchel, Controller,* v. *First National Trust and Savings Bank of San Diego* (Cal.), 190 P. 2d 611 (1948); reversing *Same,* (Cal. App.), 183 P. 2d 295 (1947).

viously for an educational purpose, said he, and even if the money were spent for frivolities it would aid education by leaving private funds free for educational uses. Thus the trust was valid.[9]

A provision, however, that the income of the trust is to be accumulated until the principal reaches $10,000, if less than that at the time of the decease of the donor, is illegal under New York law and must be excised; but this does not otherwise affect the validity of the trust.

PERFORMING THE CONDITIONS

Fisk University received by devise in 1936 some valuable real estate in Chicago, subject to only one condition: that the university stand ready to provide free tuition, room, and board for a named niece of the testatrix during a course of study leading as far as the degree of master of arts. The university trustees accepted the legacy in writing, and after the niece was graduated from high school in 1940 they repeatedly notified her of their readiness to welcome her as a student under the terms of the will. She never came, but attended another institution; and some five years later she sued, as her aunt's residuary legatee, for title to the Chicago property, an accounting for the rents collected on it by Fisk University, and $6,000 to cover the cost of her college education. Her suit was dismissed as without merit. The university had scrupulously complied with the terms of the will.[10]

In 1913–14 a donor gave to the American University in Washington, District of Columbia, some $16,000 to endow the Gustavus F. Swift fellowship, to be available only to a graduate of the Garrett Biblical Institute. It seems that for twenty-five years thereafter the successive recipients of the fellowship were not required to attend the American University, but were permitted often, if not invariably, to study at some other institu-

[9] *In re Lewis' Estate* (N.Y. Sur.), 99 N.Y.S. 2d 986 (1950).
[10] *Caruthers* v. *Fisk University* (Ill.), 68 N.E. 2d 296 (1946).

tion; but in 1942 the trustees of American University determined by resolution that thereafter the holders of the fellowship should study at American University. This was opposed by authorities of the Garrett Biblical Institute, who contended that it was the donor's intent that each beneficiary should select for himself the institution at which he would study. The facts surrounding the making of the gift did not support this contention, and the first litigation in federal district court resulted in a summary judgment sustaining the American University's position. The Court of Appeals, however, thought there was a genuine issue of material fact, and remanded the case for trial on the merits. At the conclusion of the next proceeding, District Judge Letts found in favor of the university, and said with some asperity, "It is somewhat difficult to understand what justiciable rights the defendant Institute has in the matters in issue. It was not a party to any transaction leading to the establishment of the fellowship and has performed a gratuitous service in nominating its graduates. It has no other or further interest, duty, or authority." This opinion was subsequently affirmed by the United States Court of Appeals for the District of Columbia.[11]

[11] *American University* v. *Garrett Biblical Institute* (U.S.D.C., D.C.), 84 F. Supp. 596 (1949); *affirmed* in *Garrett Biblical Institute* v. *American University* (U.S.C.A., D.C.), 181 F. 2d 866 (1950). Originally remanded for trial on the merits in *Same,* 82 U.S.C.A., D.C. 265, 163 F. 2d 265 (1947).

CHAPTER V

FACULTY MEMBERS AND OTHER EMPLOYEES: CONTRACTS AND SALARIES

THIS chapter includes cases concerning the inception, duration, and termination of contracts for personal services. Litigated controversies regarding salaries, and one relating to the concurrent extramural remunerative activities of a university dean also appear here. Cases dealing with the application of tenure statutes, retirement schemes, workmen's compensation laws, and civil service statutes are reserved for the next following chapter.

INCEPTION OF THE CONTRACT

A bacteriologist living in Pennsylvania negotiated with an institution in California regarding a position as associate professor and head of the research department of a projected institute of tropical disease. He had a physical handicap which made it necessary for him to use crutches and made it impossible for him to use stairways without assistance. He took great care to make the facts fully known in the preliminary correspondence and specifically asked if they would disqualify him.

Upon receiving a negative answer to that question and an outright offer of employment at $3,600 for the academic year of ten months, the professor accepted and presented himself at the California institution to begin work. On the second day after his arrival the president informed him that he had changed his mind and the institution paid the expenses of the professor's immediate return to his home in Pennsylvania. The facts of the case made it a clear breach of contract and at a trial occurring after the end of the academic year the professor was awarded a judgment for the full agreed salary for the entire ten months with interest on each monthly installment from the date it became due.[1]

DURATION OF THE CONTRACT

In a Missouri case a housemother had begun her employment in a dormitory at Park College in 1943. She was paid $60 a month and received her apartment and two meals a day at the dormitory table, estimated to be worth $40 a month. Customarily she was away on vacation during the month of August and communicated with the president of the college before returning to work in September. There was no written contract and no evidence of an explicit oral contract for a particular term of employment.

During the summer of 1945 there was a change in the presidency, and the new president wrote asking the housemother to return in September. She returned at the usual time and took up residence in the dormitory as formerly, but it developed that this building had no student residents, presumably on account of the wartime depletion of the student body. On October 10, the president became aware that she had no duties and asked her to assist in the other dormitories and in the hospital.

A few weeks later she was advised that her employment would be terminated at the end of the calendar year, and she received no salary payments after January 1, 1946. However, she continued to use her residence and boarding privileges at the college until April 15, when she was ousted to make her apartment available to house a student veteran and his family.

She sued for breach of contract, claiming that under the circumstances there was a contract for the full academic year. The trial court accepted this view and awarded her $560 in damages against the college—computed as her salary of $60 a month from

[1] *Canavan* v. *College of Osteopathic Physicians and Surgeons* (Cal. App.), 166 P. 2d 878 (1946).

January through July, and the value of her quarters and board ($40 a month) from April 15 through July 31. The Missouri court of appeals reversed this judgment and held that from the evidence it appeared her contract was terminable by either party at will, and neither party could be bound for a full college year or for any other fixed period of time.[2]

The comptroller of Phillips Academy, endeavoring to persuade a friend to accept employment as his assistant, was alleged to have indicated orally that "the job would last the rest of his life if he behaved himself" and that he would get a specified salary, use of a house at low rental, and retirement benefits.

The prospective assistant accordingly accepted orally and entered upon the employment in 1939. There was no written contract and no ratification by the board of trustees. In 1941 the assistant was dismissed by the treasurer, whereupon he sued the trustees as on contract for life tenure.

A directed verdict in favor of the trustees was appealed to the supreme judicial court of Massachusetts and readily sustained. It would be unreasonable to hold that the comptroller had ostensible or apparent authority to offer employment for life, thought the court. His duties were defined as "to control accounts and check expenditures." This would not include the power to employ an assistant for life. The academy had no lifetime contract with any officer or employee and no precedents of that kind. Accordingly no such contract existed here.[3]

TERMINATION OF THE CONTRACT:

DISCHARGE FOR CAUSE

An incident at a private college in Connecticut led to the summary discharge, in February 1948, of the academic dean, who had occupied his position since September 1947. In December two girl students were struck by an automobile while walking across a street in New Haven, and received minor in-

[2] *Forsyth v. Board of Trustees of Park College* (Mo. App.), 212 S.W. 2d 82 (1948).
[3] *Braden v. Trustees of Phillips Academy* (Mass.), 71 N.E. 2d 765 (1947).

juries. The president of the college advised them not to sign a paper exonerating the driver, and made a report of the accident to the insurance company carrying a group accident insurance policy covering them. A few days later the dean, on his own initiative, called police for an investigation; and in February wrote to the mothers of both girls that "the Larsons [the president of the college and his wife] will be against you in any suit, so your lawyer should be warned about them. He has admissions from both girls that they were to blame and he may try to help the driver in the hope of getting a 'handout' from him." Also there was evidence that he had written, "I accepted this position in good faith only to find that I was supposed to be merely an educational front, behind which the Larsons would continue to 'operate' as usual. Do not mistrust your daughter. She only knows one thousandth-part of the story." Disclosure of these statements was followed by immediate discharge of the dean.

After the end of the academic year he sued the college to recover the amount of his salary at $5,500 a year from the date of his discharge (February 25, 1948) to June 30, 1948, alleging breach of contract. The defense was prior breach by the plaintiff, and judgment was for the college. The Court of Errors and Appeals sustained this conclusion, declaring that the relationship of employer and employee imports trust and confidence; and if an employee intentionally does anything detrimental to the employer's interests, this constitutes a breach of the contract by the employee, and justifies his summary dismissal.[4]

An individual who had been in the employ of the Colorado School of Mines for eight years entered upon an annual contract of employment as director of physical education at a salary of $2,750 to be paid in twelve equal monthly installments from September 1, 1945, to August 31, 1946. On February 9, 1946, the board of trustees discharged him, and for services rendered up to that date paid him an aggregate of $1,601.39, being

[4] *Breen* v. *Larson College* (Conn.), 75 A. 2d 39 (1950).

"that proportion of his full annual salary which his period of service up to February 9 bears to the full school year." The cause of his discharge was the fact that he was concurrently active, at hours not conflicting with his duties at the school, as manager of a cocktail lounge in the La Ray Hotel in Golden. It appeared that he had been engaged in the same or similar business, without the knowledge of the board at the time, when his annual contract had been entered into. When the board became cognizant of these facts, it informed him, "You must give up your employment in connection with the dispensing of liquors if you wish to remain on the faculty at this institution."

After the close of the academic year he sued for the remainder of his annual salary as on breach of contract, and was awarded a judgment for $1,148.61 in the trial court. The supreme court of Colorado remanded the case with direction to vacate the judgment, and in lieu thereof to adjudge recovery in only a *nominal* sum, together with costs. This result was reached because there was in the record an admission by him that following his discharge he had made much more money operating the Golden Nugget Cafe and in other remunerative activities than he would have been paid under the contract.

Chief Justice Hilliard remarked: "None will say, we think, that moral justification did not attend the action of the trustees in the premises." But since there was no complaint of failure of the athletic director to perform duties required under his contract with the school, he had a right to sue, after the expiration of the contract term, for damages. The measure of damages in such cases, however, is only nominal under Colorado precedents, when it appears that the plaintiff has actually suffered no pecuniary loss as a result of his discharge.[5]

SALARIES

The Kentucky Constitution of 1891 provides that no public officer except the governor shall receive more than $5,000 a year

[5] *Colorado School of Mines* v. *Neighbors et al.* (Colo.), 203 P. 2d 904 (1949).

as official compensation. A decade or more ago this began to cramp the university and state colleges regarding the positions of presidents, deans, and senior professors. For a time certain salaries at the University of Kentucky were lawfully supplemented out of funds from private sources. In 1942 the question of whether the constitutional limitation properly applied to university salaries was put squarely to the Kentucky court of appeals, and the court, with only Justice Rees dissenting, declared that, although university professors and administrators are employees of the state and are not public officers, yet the clause must be construed to include, by inference, not only public officers but all public employees as well.

A proposal to amend that clause of the constitution was submitted to the voters and failed to carry at the polls in 1943; and the question of the interpretation of the clause again reached the highest court of the state late in 1947. This time the majority of the court adopted the view of Justice Rees, overruled the pertinent parts of its former decision, and decided that the ceiling on salaries of "public officers" should be construed to mean precisely what it says and no more, and not extended by implication to embrace employees of the state who are admittedly not "public officers." [6] Therefore, it is not properly applicable to the salaries of state university and college professors, deans, and presidents. Chief Justice Sims and Justice Thomas joined in a dissent, arguing that, in view of the history of the clause in recent years, it should be amended, if at all, only by vote of the people and not by judicial interpretation.

In New York, a statute known as the Moffat Act of 1943 embodies a salary schedule for teachers at City College of the City of New York and at Brooklyn College. A portion of the act, being Section 3104, New York Education Law, is interpreted as making specified salary increments for full professors *mandatory* until they have attained an annual salary of $7,500, and *discretionary* thereafter until a maximum of $9,600 is reached.

[6] *Pardue et al.* v. *Miller*, Commissioner of Finance (Ky.), 206 S.W. 2d 75 (1947).

Disputing this interpretation, certain litigants recently petitioned under Section 1283 of the Civil Practice Act to compel the Board of Higher Education to construe the increments as mandatory up to $9,600, to adjust the petitioners' pay accordingly, and to award back pay representing the difference. The petition was denied in the trial court, upon evidence that under the practice of the Board begun in 1935, *mandatory* increments did not go above $7,500; and the intent of the act of 1943 was to codify the previous practice of the board in that respect. Moreover, Judge Eder thought the fact that all parties concerned had acquiesced in that interpretation for more than four years after the act became effective was sufficient to estop the petitioners and others similarly situated from asserting that the Board's application of the statute is erroneous or illegal.[7]

CONCURRENT EXTRAMURAL ACTIVITIES

The perennially recurrent question of extramural remunerative activities of faculty members appeared in the suit of a taxpayer to recover for the state $14,374.93 paid as salary to the dean of the College of Engineering at the University of Kentucky during nearly three years, 1941–44, while he was in Washington as consultant to the Assistant Chief of Staff of the Army (two years) at $1 a year, and adviser to the Under Secretary of War (one year) at $8,000 a year. Upon conclusive evidence that during the entire period he performed the "full function of the office of dean," with an assistant dean acting under his direction in his absence, and that in addition he "rendered extraordinary services to the university which otherwise would have required the president, or some other representative of the university, to make many and frequent trips to Washington," the court decided that the services "were well worth the salary paid him by the university." [8]

[7] *Otis et al.* v. *Board of Higher Education of City of New York et al.* (Misc.), 97 N.Y.S. 2d 600 (1950).

[8] *Commonwealth ex rel. Harper et al.* v. *Graham et al.* (Ky.), 194 S.W. 2d 377 (1946).

CHAPTER VI

TENURE, RETIREMENT, WORKMEN'S COMPENSATION, CIVIL SERVICE STATUTES

THE preceding chapter looks at contracts largely from the common-law viewpoint. The conditions of employment in universities and colleges are also often affected by statutes or institutional ordinances regarding tenure and retirement. Coverage of some or all institutional employees under state workmen's compensation laws and civil service statutes also occasionally gives rise to litigation. Such cases are grouped here.

TENURE

A California statute of August 4, 1943, provided that any teacher in the state colleges reappointed after three consecutive years of prior service would be considered appointed on indefinite tenure, and created a board of appeals. A professor of chemistry at San Jose State College, who had been reappointed June 30, 1943, was notified on December 6 of that year that his job would be abolished and his employment terminated June 30, 1944. He sued unsuccessively for a writ of mandate to compel the board of appeals to review his case. The board had no jurisdiction, because the act creating it was prospective and not retractive; and the professor's last reappointment had occurred before the act became effective.[1]

That the position of a teacher possessing indefinite tenure cannot be abolished retroactively was shown in a case at the College of the City of New York, where the governing board

[1] *Botts* v. *Simpson* (Cal. App.), 167 P. 2d 231 (1946).

adopted a resolution October 18, 1943, declaring a particular position as teacher of stenography and typewriting to be excess and purporting to abolish it retroactively as of September 1, 1943. The teacher had been available during the intervening seven-week period and was, therefore, entitled to her full salary for that period.[2]

Some hardship to teachers on permanent tenure in the Townsend Harris High School (preparatory school at City College, New York City) was occasioned when that school was closed in 1942 and their jobs abolished. They were put on a preferred eligible list for three years, but *not* eligible for positions in City College or any of the other municipal colleges. One such teacher who had been in Townsend Harris since 1923, and had acquired permanent tenure in 1931, was employed after 1942 in certain temporary capacities at City College. He sued for a declaration that he was a regular member of the City College faculty with tenure rights from 1931, and lost his case. Acceptance of temporary appointments in the college was a waiver of tenure; a decision of 1942 had held that Townsend Harris was a separate noncollege institution; and a letter from the president of City College purporting to give the plaintiff certain voting rights in faculty meetings was probably not intended to affect his tenure status, and was beyond the president's authority if it was so intended.[3]

RETIREMENT

The Board of Governors of West Virginia University, by an order adopted in 1935, provided that faculty members upon passing the age of 65 be placed on limited service status, with annual stipends of $1,200 to $1,800. In 1941 a state teachers' retirement act was enacted, including university teachers in its coverage, and providing small retirement allowances. There-

[2] *Miranda* v. *Tead et al., Board of Higher Education,* 295 N.Y. 545, 68 N.E. 2d 682 (1946).

[3] *Trilling* v. *Board of Higher Education of City of New York et al.* (Misc.), 67 N.Y.S. 2d 572 (1946).

after the university paid to its retired faculty members the difference between their former annual stipends and their annual retirement allowances under the act of 1941. When the payment of these sums out of funds appropriated by the legislature to the university for personal services was questioned by the state auditor, the supreme court of West Virginia decided that such payments were contrary to the constitution and unlawful. Therefore it refused to issue a writ of *mandamus* to compel the state auditor to honor requisitions for the payment of these stipends out of funds appropriated for the biennium 1947–49. It appeared that the recipients of stipends did not, and were not expected to perform any work for the university.

Noting that this retirement plan was without statutory authorization, the court pointed to Article VI, Section 38, West Virginia Constitution: ". . . nor shall any legislature authorize the payment of any claim or part thereof, hereafter created against the state, under any agreement or contract made, without express authority of law; and all such unauthorized agreements shall be null and void." There was no inherent power in the Board of Governors of the university to make the payments or agree to make them, thought the court. Said Justice Fox:

> The profession of teaching is a high and honorable vocation, but teachers in our university cannot, through any theory of implication, be singled out as entitled to favors which, under the law, cannot be granted to worthy employees of the State Board of Control, who handle our humane and penal institutions, or teachers in our schools of higher learning other than the university, which are placed within the control of the State Board of Education.[4]

WORKMEN'S COMPENSATION

University employees are often covered by the workmen's compensation laws providing awards in case of death or injury incurred in the course of their duties. A housemother of a

[4] *State ex rel. Board of Governors of West Virginia University* v. *Sims* (W. Va.), 55 S.E. 2d 505 (1949).

girls' dormitory at the University of Idaho fell on a slippery sidewalk in Moscow in the winter of 1943, fracturing her femur, and four days later she died of a cerebral hemorrhage. She occupied a suite with kitchenette in the cooperative dormitory, and was regarded as on duty twenty-four hours a day. She prepared her own breakfast, buying and paying for the food thus used, and from time to time as part of her duties she invited girls into her suite for coffee or light refreshments, to make the dormitory homelike for them and to cure cases of homesickness or mental depression. When she suffered the fatal accident, she was on the errand of buying coffee for that use, and also some Christmas tree ornaments for a celebration planned by the residents of the dormitory. Affirming an award of compensation to her heir-at-law, the Idaho supreme court said: "Mrs. Smith was discharging a duty incident to the nature of her employment and in the interest and for the benefit of her employer; therefore the injury sustained by her is compensable." [5]

In Michigan the workmen's compensation act of 1912 was amended in 1913 to provide compulsory coverage, as employers, of "the state, and each county, city, township, incorporated village and school district therein, and each incorporated public board or public commission in the state authorized by law to hold property and to sue and be sued generally. . . ." The governing board of the Michigan State College of Agriculture and Applied Science is clearly within the quoted definition, but the question of whether the act can apply to it is particularly difficult because of the well-established principle that this institution is a constitutionally independent corporation having a large sphere of freedom from control by the legislature, under the constitution of Michigan.

When an employee of the college filed a claim with the Compensation Commission for a personal injury sustained in 1946, the college answered that, not having so elected, it is not subject to the workmen's compensation act. The trial court declined

[5] *Smith* v. *University of Idaho, et al.* (Ida.), 170 P. 2d 404 (1946).

to sustain this view, and ordered the case remanded to the commission to be heard on the merits. This order was affirmed by the supreme court of Michigan; but so difficult was the decision that the eight justices participating were evenly divided, four to four. In such an event, the judgment of the lower court is affirmed. The opinion which thus prevails was written by Justice Reid, with Chief Justice Bushnell and Justices Sharpe and Butzel concurring. The rationale of the decision is that the enactment of the workmen's compensation law is an exercise of the state's police power; that the constitution vests no part of the police power in the governing board of the college; that the police power of the state is to be exercised by the legislature.

The dissenting opinion was by Justice Dethmers, with Justices Boyles, North, and Carr joining. It maintains that

> the employment of persons for the prosecution of college business, functions or operations is within the defendant's exclusive supervision; the payment of compensation, from college funds, in the event of personal injury arising out of and in the course of such employment involves an act of direction and control of agricultural college funds which . . . is within the exclusive power of the defendant board.[6]

CIVIL SERVICE STATUTES

In some states the nonteaching employees of state colleges and universities are within the purview of state civil service laws. An Arizona act of 1948 which would have accomplished that result was held unconstitutional and void. Said Justice Windes, for the unanimous supreme court of Arizona:

> The plain meaning of this is that all employees of educational institutions maintained or supported by the state, except members of teaching staffs, fall within the classified civil service under the supervision of the civil service board and its personnel officer. The board of regents of the university and state colleges, as *amicus curiae,* calls our attention to Article 11, Section 2, Arizona Constitution: "The general conduct and supervision of the public school system shall

[6] *Peters* v. *Michigan State College et al.*, 320 Mich. 243, 30 N.W. 2d 854 (1948).

be vested in a state board of education, a state superintendent of public instruction, . . . and such governing boards for the state institutions as may be provided by law."

Clearly this means that our schools, including the educational institutions supported by the state, such as the university and state colleges, are to be under the supervision of special governing boards. . . . To permit legislation to throw the employment and supervision of all personnel under the civil service law, except the teaching staff, would necessarily deprive the board of regents of a large portion of its constitutional supervisory power. We have no hesitation in holding that such legislation runs counter to said Article 11, Section 2, Arizona Constitution.[7]

[7] *Hernandez* v. *Frohmiller,* 68 Ariz. 242, 204 P. 2d 854 (1949).

PART TWO

STATE AND MUNICIPAL INSTITUTIONS

CHAPTER VII

THE LEGAL POSITION OF STATE COLLEGES AND UNIVERSITIES

HAVE any new developments extended or modified the concept of the constitutionally independent state institution of higher education? What do the recent decisions show regarding the degree to which state university governing boards are circumscribed by statutory controls? Is the board of regents of a state university system within its rights in operating a cut-rate laundry service for the benefit of students and other persons connected with an institution under its management? Can rulings of the Federal Communications Commission prevent the enforcement of a contract by a state educational institution to buy or sell a radio broadcasting station?

CONSTITUTIONAL INDEPENDENCE

The state universities in Michigan, Minnesota, California, Idaho, Colorado, and Utah continue to have the dignity of fourth coordinate arms of the state government, as do the separate land-grant colleges in Michigan, Oklahoma, and Utah. Added to this company of constitutionally independent corporations is the Board of Regents of the University System of Georgia (pages 37–38, *The Colleges and the Courts, 1941–1945*). In 1948 and 1949 decisions in Nevada and Arizona enunciated and upheld certain constitutional prerogatives of the governing boards of state institutions of higher education.

In Arizona it was held that the Board of Regents of the University and State Colleges, created by legislative act pursuant to Article 11, Section 2 of the state constitution, is vested by the constitution with a sphere of authority such that its power to appoint and supervise the employees of the institutions under its jurisdiction can not be infringed upon to the extent of making these employees subject to a state civil service system. Thus an act of 1948, enacted by popular initiative, creating a state civil service system in which nonteaching employees of the state university and state colleges would be embraced, was declared for that reason and to that extent unconstitutional and void.[1]

Two decisions of the same court in 1946 and 1949 also reaffirmed the principle that in Arizona the state auditor can not interpose a discretionary authority as to the disbursement of funds which have been appropriated to or have otherwise come into the control of the board of regents, and are obligated for public purposes. Thus the state auditor was judicially commanded to issue warrants covering vouchers for institutional membership fees in educational and other learned and scientific associations, and for travel expenses of institutional representatives attending meetings and conferences of such bodies; [2] and vouchers for expenses incurred for the ceremonial inauguration of a new president of the University of Arizona.[3]

A Nevada act of 1947 creating an advisory board to the Board of Regents of the University of Nevada was declared unconstitutional and void in a two to one decision of the state supreme court in 1948. The theory of the decision, from which Chief Justice Eather dissented, is that the board of regents owes its existence to the state constitution, and the legislature can not create a duplicate body to perform the duties of a constitutional office.[4]

The invalid act would have created an "advisory board of

1 *Hernandez* v. *Frohmiller*, 68 Ariz. 242, 204 P. 2d 854 (1949).

2 *Frohmiller* v. *Board of Regents of University and State Colleges* (Ariz.), 171 P. 2d 356 (1946).

3 *Board of Regents of University and State Colleges* v. *Frohmiller*, 69 Ariz. 50, 208 P. 2d 833 (1949).

4 *King* v. *Board of Regents of University of Nevada* (Nev.), 200 P. 2d 221 (1948).

regents" of not more than seven members, to be nominated by the Board of Regents itself and appointed by the governor. These "advisory regents" would have "all the rights and privileges, including travel and incidental expenses, of the elected Regents but shall not have a determining vote on any matter properly under the control of the elected Board of Regents." Section 4 of the act declared: "No provision of this act shall be construed to be in derogation of the constitutional authority of the elected Board of Regents to administer the affairs of the university." But this could not save it, in the eyes of the majority of the court. Justice Badt, with Justice Horsey concurring, concluded in a 12,000-word opinion that

> It was the intention of the framers of the constitution to vest exclusive executive and administrative control of the university in a board of regents to be elected by the people; and the act creating the advisory board would change, alter or modify its constitutional powers and functions and cannot find its justification in the power of the legislature to define the duties of the elected board.

In the course of the opinion considerable attention was given to the leading cases on the constitutional independence of state institutions of higher education in Michigan, Minnesota, Idaho, and Oklahoma; and a paragraph by Justice Badt goes far to clarify a popular misconception regarding the relation between a state legislature and a constitutionally created state university:

> Respondent insists that the unquestioned right of the legislature to appropriate the required funds for maintaining the university indicates that the elected board of regents was not vested by the constitution with exclusive and plenary control. However, the two processes are distinct. The power of the legislature to provide the requisite money and to limit and decrease the amount considered by the regents to be necessary is entirely a different function from the administration and control of the university itself.

The issue of the constitutional independence of the University of Utah and of the Utah State Agricultural College entered somewhat obliquely into a decision of the Utah supreme court sustaining the validity of an $850,000 bond issue by the agricultural college to finance a new student union building. One argument before the court challenged the *de jure* status of the governing board of the agricultural college, in view of the fact that its composition has been changed by the state legislature subsequent to the adoption of the state constitution containing a clause confirming and perpetuating the powers and franchises of the two institutions as they existed at that time. This question is reminiscent of the significant Minnesota case of *State ex rel. Peterson* v. *Quinlivan* (Minn.), 268 N.W. 858 (1936), in which, under a similar clause, the composition of the governing board of the University of Minnesota was held to be beyond the power of the legislature to change.

The Utah court reached the opposite conclusion (in a majority opinion of three of the five justices), and held that the constitution did not "freeze" the composition of the governing board of the agricultural college. Deeming this sufficient to support the *de jure* character of the present composition of the board, the court went no further: "We need not and do not pass on the right of the legislature to deal with any other or different rights, immunities, franchises or endowments which might have been granted to the college by the Constitution." [5] Two justices who concurred in approving the bond issue thought that result could be reached without opening the question of constitutional independence. Thus in the present case the whole question of constitutional independence was not squarely before the court, and was expressly not fully decided.

INTERPOSITION OF THE STATE'S POLICE POWER

We have noticed in an earlier chapter that the Michigan State College of Agriculture and Applied Science, though it has consistently been held to have a wide sphere of independence under the constitution of Michigan, is, as a result of a tie vote of the

[5] *Spence* v. *Utah State Agricultural College* (Utah), 225 P. 2d 18 (1950).

eight justices of the supreme court in 1948, subject to the statewide Workmen's Compensation Act. The votes of four of the justices to affirm a lower court decision to that effect were based on the theory that the Workmen's Compensation Act is an exercise of the state's police power (concerned with the health and safety of the public), and that in this field the legislature is supreme. The other four justices maintained that the exclusive control of college funds which is vested by the constitution in the college governing board should preclude any compulsory payments of college funds to injured employees.[6]

EXTENT OF CONTROL BY THE LEGISLATURE

Without reference to any sphere of constitutional independence, what may an institutional governing board do or not do without specific statutory authorization? A few varying examples from different states follow.

The Arkansas State Hospital at Little Rock is on a site of 160 acres. Some thirty acres of the site have never been needed or used for hospital purposes. The medical school of the University of Arkansas occupies a single city block in Little Rock, a site insufficient to accommodate the plant expansion authorized by a legislative act of 1947 and provided for by a state appropriation of $1,600,000 and a federal grant of $800,000. In these circumstances the state hospital and the university negotiated an agreement under which the hospital would give the university a suitable part of the hospital grounds to be used as a site for the new university memorial hospital and medical school; the university would erect its new medical school and hospital plant accordingly; and the state hospital and the state university would thus gain many mutual advantages. Medical students would gain by having an abundance of clinical material in nervous and mental diseases accesible at the adjacent state hospital. State-hospital patients would gain by having a general hospital and medical center immediately at hand. The state would get a

[6] *Peters* v. *Michigan State College et al.*, 320 Mich. 243, 30 N.W. 2d 854 (1948).

large and modern medical plant and equipment with economy of expenditure and a minimum of duplication of facilities.

In October 1947 the state hospital board, meeting in Little Rock, voted to grant the site; and two days later the trustees of the University of Arkansas, meeting at the university campus in Fayetteville, voted to accept the grant and proceed accordingly. Thereupon a taxpayer sued to enjoin the acts of both boards, alleging that they had exceeded their powers and set themselves up unlawfully as vested with powers which belong only to the state legislature. The Arkansas supreme court readily sustained the boards and affirmed the denial of the injunction. Finding no explicit statutory authority for the joint plan, the court pointed out that none is necessary, for boards of trustees not only have all powers specifically delegated, but also such additional or implied powers as may be necessary to carry out the trust to the best advantage of the public. Also, as to the university board of trustees, statutory authority to construct buildings carries with it by implication power to acquire sites.[7]

Although the practice of obtaining specific statutory authority for the financing of self-liquidating college or university buildings has been almost universal among the states, there are exceptions. For example, the supreme court of Missouri recently held that in view of the postwar student-housing stringency at the University of Missouri, the Board of Curators could lawfully proceed to borrow money for the erection of self-liquidating dormitories without any specific statutory authorization.[8]

On the other hand, a 1949 decision in West Virginia strikes down a rudimentary noncontributory retirement system for faculty members at West Virignia University, which was initiated in 1935 by the Board of Governors of the university without statutory authority, and in which small retirement allowances were paid out of funds appropriated to the university by the legislature for personal services. The court pointed to a

[7] *Lindsay* v. *White, et al.* (Ark.), 206 S.W. 2d 762 (1947).

[8] *Curators of University of Missouri* v. *McReynolds* (Mo.), 193 S.W. 2d 611 (1946).

clause in the state constitution which forbids payment of any claim against the state "without express authority of law" and nullifies any agreement to the contrary.[9]

OPERATING NECESSARY SERVICE ENTERPRISES

Certain proprietors of commercial laundry and dry-cleaning establishments sought to enjoin the Board of Regents of the University System of Georgia from furnishing laundry and dry-cleaning services at reduced prices for persons connected with the Georgia State College for Women at Milledgeville. The petitioners argued that the service should be confined solely to work for boarding students and institutional flatwork, and should exclude members of the Board of Regents, executives, faculty members, other employees, and all their families. In support of this contention, several arguments were adduced, all without success. To the far-fetched assertion that the obligations necessarily incurred in the laundry service were unconstitutional "debts against the state," the court replied by pointing to a leading Georgia decision of 1934, of which the syllabus says:

> The Regents of the University System of Georgia is a distinct corporate entity and is governed by a Board of Regents. Through the board it can exercise any power usually granted to such incorporations, necessary to its usefulness, and not in conflict with the Constitution and laws. An obligation incurred by the corporation, or the Board of Regents, is not a debt of the state, and therefore is not affected by constitutional limitations upon state indebtedness.[10]

A particular target was a member of the Board of Regents who was alleged to be having his laundry done at cost at the college laundry. This, said the court, would not be a violation of the statute which limits the compensation of members of the Board of Regents to $7 a day and transportation. Brushing aside the tenuous contention that the operation of the college laundry

[9] *State ex rel. Board of Governors of West Virginia University* v. *Sims* (W. Va.), 55 S.E. 2d 505 (1949).

[10] *State* v. *Regents,* 179 Ga. 210, 175 S.E. 567 (1934).

amounted to a "taking of property without due process" from commercial competitors, the court remarked that an entrepreneur in business is not guaranteed a monopoly. The conclusion was that the complaint stated no cause of action.[11]

A somewhat similar controversy at another institution controlled by the same board is digested in Chapter XXI, entitled "Accessory Educational Corporations," because in that case the laundry service was operated by an incorporated athletic association.

RELATION TO LOCAL TAXING AUTHORITIES

The perennial argument about the plight of the local political subdivision that has a large tax-free institution within its boundaries goes on.

In a sort of omnibus complaint, asking somewhat incoherently for many remedies, a citizen and taxpayer of Ann Arbor sued on behalf of himself and other taxpayers, asking that the city be compelled to tax the property of the University of Michigan within its jurisdiction; that the property be placed on the local tax rolls; that the regents of the university be compelled to contract with the city for fire and police protection, street maintenance, and sanitary services; and that an accounting be had for the cost of these services furnished by the city to the university over the last forty years.

The contention was that the city is now, and has been for many years, giving free fire and police protection and other services to the property of the university, the reasonable value of such services being something like $200,000 a year; and that the university holds tax-free some $20,000,000 worth of buildings and other facilities not used for educational purposes exclusively and therefore unquestionably taxable.

The Washtenaw circuit court dismissed the complaint, and this judgment was affirmed by the supreme court of Michigan.

11 *Villyard et al. v. Regents of University System of Georgia* (Ga.), 50 S.E. 2d 313 (1948).

The reasons for this conclusion were multiple. In the first place, the property of the university is property of the state, and the suit was consequently essentially a suit against the state. A historic principle of Anglo-Saxon law makes the state immune from suit unless it gives its permission to be sued.

Not wishing to invoke this somewhat arbitrary device as the sole support of its judgment, however, the court stated other reasons. Noting carefully that the suit was brought by an individual, and not by or on behalf of the city, the judge said:

> The court in chancery cannot substitute its judgment for that of the proper municipal authorities, or the board of regents, as to whether taxes should be levied or contracts entered into to provide for the furnishing of police facilities by the city. We are unable to conclude from the facts and circumstances alleged in appellant's bill of complaint that either the appellant or the taxpayers of the city of Ann Arbor are being deprived of property without due process of law.

Specifically on the question of payments under contract in lieu of taxes, the tribunal concluded, "It is not for the court to consider the propriety of a contract between the city of Ann Arbor and the board of regents, for the city to furnish police or fire protection or other public facilities for state property within the corporate limits." [12]

SALE AND PURCHASE OF RADIO STATIONS: RULES OF FEDERAL COMMUNICATIONS COMMISSION

The Regents of the New Mexico College of Agriculture and Mechanic Arts in 1936 sold the physical assets of Station KOB to the Albuquerque Broadcasting Company, and assigned the operating license to the purchaser for $25,000 cash and the use of the station one hour per day for educational purposes. The agreement stipulated that the selection of the particular hour of the day should be at the option of the college, but also that the broadcasting company should have "complete control" of

[12] *Lucking* v. *People* (Mich.), 31 N.W. 2d 707 (1948).

programming. This ambiguity gave rise to some difficulties, which became acute in 1945 when the college demanded the use of the station four and one-half hours per week, at specified hours, in addition to the time then being used in accord with the contract of sale. Thereupon the broadcasting company sued for a declaratory judgment to determine its rights. The federal District Court held that the company could not lawfully accede to the college's demand, because, as licensee, the company has the legal duty "to choose, select, and schedule programs in the interest of the listening public." Performance of this duty, however, "is subject to review by the Federal Communications Commission in a proper proceeding under Sections 309 or 312 of the Federal Communications Act," and "defendant [the college] can always invoke the administrative discretion of that agency if it is of the opinion that plaintiff [the company] is not broadcasting defendant's programs that are in the interest of the listening public." [13]

The Regents of the University System of Georgia purchased, for the Georgia Institute of Technology, Station WGST at Atlanta from the stockholders of "Southern Broadcasting Stations, Inc." The Regents agreed to pay therefor "15 per cent of the net billings" of the station, from April 15, 1943, to January 6, 1950. The payments were made until July 1945, when they were stopped; and the stockholders sued in the state courts for breach of contract. The Regents' defense was that under rulings of the Federal Communications Commission the station could not be licensed with that clause of the contract in force, and that therefore performance was "excused by act of law." In behalf of the Regents it was also argued that performance of the contract so crippled the financial ability of the station as to deter it from entering into the new fields of frequency modulation and television broadcasting, and was thus contrary to the public interest. The trial court held that the contract was enforceable as a pri-

[13] *Albuquerque Broadcasting Company* v. *Regents of New Mexico College of Agriculture and Mechanic Arts* (U.S.D.C.), 70 F. Supp. 198 (1945).

vate agreement; that the Federal Communications Commission does not regulate the private affairs of licensees; and ordered the Regents to pay 15 percent of the billings from July 1945 to the date of the suit, aggregating $144,968.63 plus $10,991.31 in accrued interest. This judgment was affirmed by a Georgia court of appeals, after transfer of the case by the supreme court of Georgia. The court was influenced by the contention that "the Regents, being a state governmental agency, have been relieved from the payment of certain taxes, including income taxes, and this amounts to an increase in the income received by the station from its operation in excess of or equal to the 15 per cent of the net billings," and declared that it could not be anticipated that the contract would so far affect the financial ability of the station as to render it unable to operate in the public interest.

This decision was reviewed and affirmed by the United States Supreme Court in an opinion written by Mr. Justice Reed. He put the federal question clearly: "The Federal Communications Commission . . . renewed a radio license only after the . . . Board of Regents carried out a required repudiation of a contract. . . . May a state now enforce the repudiated contract . . . although this would have the practical effect of nullifying the repudiation required by the Commission?" He concluded that a correct conception of the relation between federal administrative power and state judicial power compels an affirmative answer. Moreover, said he, "The Commission has said frequently that controversies as to rights between licensees and others are outside the ambit of its powers." Pointing out that in this case the Commission was satisfied that the contract was of "no effect" when the Board of Regents made a unilateral disaffirmance of it, he conceded that "This choice of method lay within the Commission's power." [14]

[14] *Regents of University System of Georgia et al.* v. *Carroll et al.*, 78 Ga. App. 292, 50 S.E. 2d 808 (1948); appeal transferred, 203 Ga. 292, 46 S.E. 2d 496 (1948); affirmed, *Same*, 70 S. Ct. 370 (1950).

PART THREE

PRIVATELY CONTROLLED INSTITUTIONS

CHAPTER VIII

SOME RELATIONSHIPS OF PRIVATELY CONTROLLED INSTITUTIONS TO THE STATES

THE cases under this rubric are of two types: (1) those involving judicial superintendence of educational corporations, and (2) those concerned with the power of the state to license private and professional schools. These cases are grouped because they are close to the essence of the legal position of privately controlled colleges and universities in the United States. Many other facets of this position are involved in numerous other cases digested in this volume, especially in the chapters dealing with tax exemptions and with the creation and operation of educational trusts.

COURT SUPERVISION OF PRIVATE COLLEGES

The supreme court of North Carolina approved a trilateral contract whereby Wake Forest College agreed to move to a site in or near Winston-Salem and build a plant to accommodate 2,000 students; the Baptist State Convention agreed to maintain the same relationship to the college as in the past, and to pay it annually a proportion of the Convention funds not less than the proportion paid during the calendar year 1946; and the Z. Smith Reynolds Foundation agreed to pay to the college all its own income up to $350,000 not later than 1952 for expenses of moving and building, and thereafter each year all its net income up to $350,000 annually. Said the court, in deciding the friendly suit: "Wake Forest College has had a long and honorable career. . . . We should not deny to this great institution

. . . this vista of a new dawn and this vision of a new hope." [1]

A memento of the postwar period of the late 1940s is the ruling of a New York court denying an application for dissolution brought by the trustees of the New York Law School. Noting that the school had been in continuous operation since 1897, the court said:

This law school has the dignity of age and the satisfaction of nearly half a century of work well done. Among its graduates are men of extraordinary distinction. It should not be permanently discontinued at a time when it is a matter of common knowledge that thousands of young men are not able to obtain or to continue their legal education because of the limited capacity of the present law schools in this vicinity.

It suggested, however, that the way would be open for a later application if the trustees continued of the same mind after further study.[2]

STATE LICENSING OF SCHOOLS OF THE HEALING ARTS IN NEW JERSEY

A New Jersey statute for the regulation of the practice of medicine treats all "healing arts" as an entity, and requires all aspirant practitioners to have a standard education in medicine and surgery. Practitioners of healing arts and schools for their professional education are required to be licensed by the State Board of Medical Examiners. The constitutionality of these provisions was upheld by the New Jersey Court of Errors and Appeals in the 1934 case of *College of Mecca of Chiropractic* v. *State Board of Medical Examiners,* digested at page 198 in *The Colleges and the Courts* (1936).[3] A dozen years later chiropractors and naturopaths carried the controversy into a federal district court, but without success. The statute, argued the plaintiffs, makes it impossible for a school of chiropractic to ex-

[1] *Z. Smith Reynolds Foundation, Inc.* v. *Trustees of Wake Forest College, et al.* (N.C.), 42 S.E. 2d 910 (1947).

[2] *Application of New York Law School* (Misc.), 68 N.Y.S. 2d 839 (1946).

[3] Cited as 113 N.J.L. 327, 174 A. 562 (1934).

ist or operate in New Jersey, and likewise precludes the licensing of a practitioner of chiropractic or naturopathy in that state, regardless of the fact that he may be duly licensed in several other states. In fact, a chiropractor bearing licenses to practice in two other states, and having actually practiced for ten years in the town of Perth Amboy, was, at the time, being prosecuted for practicing a healing art without a license. Accordingly the plaintiffs asked the federal court to enjoin the state courts from continuing with criminal proceedings under the act, and requested a declaratory judgment that the act is unconstitutional. Neither of these prayers could be granted. Federal courts ordinarily have no jurisdiction over the enforcement of state statutes, and do not interfere with state courts in criminal proceedings. Where the constitutionality of a statute is involved, the appeal from state courts is direct to the United States Supreme Court, and not to an inferior federal court, as in this case. Therefore the complaints were dismissed. The scholarly opinion by District Judge Forman affords a compact review of numerous decisions of the Supreme Court of the United States on the constitutionality of state statutes regulating the practice of the professions and the operation of professional schools.[4]

LICENSING OF PRIVATE SCHOOLS IN NEW YORK

Section 5001 of the New York Education Law makes the Commissioner of Education's approval of the tuition fees to be charged one of the requisites for the issuance of a license to operate a trade school. A 1950 Appellate Division decision, by vote of three of the judges against two, holds that section unconstitutional and void. Plaintiff was a beauty culture school in operation since 1938. After nine years of approval of the school's operation, in 1947 the Commissioner of Education expressly disapproved certain fees being charged for lockers, notebooks, and various certificates. When the school refused to discontinue the

[4] *New Jersey Chiropractic Association et al.* v. *State Board of Medical Examiners of New Jersey et al.; New Jersey State Society of Naturopaths et al.* v. *Same* (U.S.D.C.), 79 F. Supp. 327 (1948).

fees, he denied it a license for the year 1949–50. The trial court sustained the Commissioner, but the Appellate Division reversed the decision and ordered that a license be issued forthwith.[5]

The majority opinion, in which Judges Deyo, Brewster, and Bergan joined, seems to exemplify a markedly conservative, if not reactionary, social viewpoint. Said they: "Power to fix prices, and tuition is nothing more than that, is justifiable, if at all, only as an exercise of the inherent police power of the state." They then concede that the state must have power to regulate schools "lest untrained and improperly prepared technicians be foisted upon an unsuspecting public," but follow immediately with an astonishing assertion: "What that embryo technician, be he hair stylist or masseur, dentist or doctor, may have paid for his education is purely a personal matter between himself and the school of his choice, in which the public has no proper concern."

The dissent, by Presiding Judge Foster with Judge Heffernan joining, is based on a trenchant statement:

> The legislation involved is not beyond the police power of the state. To my mind a trade school for the teaching of beauty culture in this day and generation is a business at least as much "clothed with the public interest" as a theatre or place of amusement. . . . Hence I think it a proper subject for regulation.

Another section of the New York Education Law was declared unconstitutional and invalid by the highest court of the state in 1948. A part of the statutes relating to compulsory school attendance, this section forbade anyone other than the public school authorities or an established religious group to operate a nursery school, kindergarten, or elementary school unless registered under regulations provided by the state department of education (Board of Regents of the University of the State of New York).

Packer Collegiate Institute, a private nonsectarian school for girls from nursery school through junior college, operated for

[5] *Grow System School by the Garford Lab., Inc.* v. *Board of Regents of University of State of New York* (App. Div.), 98 N.Y.S. 834 (1950).

many years in Brooklyn, was admittedly eligible for registration, but elected to refuse it and challenge the constitutionality of the law. The statute was upheld by a decision of the Appellate Division, but this judgment was reversed by the Court of Appeals, by vote of five judges against two. In the majority opinion, Judge Desmond declared the statute invalid solely because, in his view, it delegated legislative power to an administrative authority, without any accompanying standards or guides provided by the legislature. Four of the judges concurred, of whom one, Judge Fuld, went further and asserted his belief that the statute would deny nonsectarian private schools the equal protection of the laws guaranteed under the Constitution of the United States.[6]

Judge Lewis entered a dissenting opinion (in which Judge Thacher concurred), arguing that in complex and technical fields such as education it is impracticable for the legislature to go into detail, and it is therefore necessary to delegate authority broadly to administrative authorities.

[6] *Packer Collegiate Institute* v. *University of State of New York et al.*, 298 N.Y. 184, 81 N.E. 80 (1948); reversing *Same*, 273 App. Div. 203, 76 N.Y.S. 2d 499 (1948).

PART FOUR

FISCAL RELATIONSHIPS WITH GOVERNMENTAL UNITS

CHAPTER IX

STATE APPROPRIATIONS AND INSTITUTIONAL EXPENDITURES

STATE appropriations of public money are always an important factor in the support of state universities and colleges. These institutions receive, however, substantial funds from other sources, such as student fees, endowment income, federal subventions, sales of products, and operation of various auxiliary enterprises necessary to make the institution and its community a safe and convenient dwelling place. Sometimes the custody and use of these funds are in dispute. There is also the recurrent question of the constitutionality of statutes authorizing the allocation of public funds or the use of public property in aid of private nonsectarian or denominational educational institutions.

CONSTITUTIONAL INTERDICTION IN OKLAHOMA

In 1945 the Oklahoma legislature established the Southern Oklahoma Hospital at Ardmore, made it "auxiliary to the University Hospital," and placed it under the control of the board of regents of the University of Oklahoma at Norman. In two other separate acts at the same session the legislature made a direct appropriation of money to the Southern Oklahoma Hospital and memorialized the Oklahoma State Regents for Higher Education to allocate funds to it. Now a section of the state constitution forbids the legislature to make a specific appropriation to a particular institution under the jurisdiction of the state regents and provides that all such institutions shall receive funds only as allocated by the state regents from a lump sum appropriated to the state regents by the legislature.

Clearly, then, the direct legislative appropriation to the hospital was unconstitutional and void, and the state treasurer could not be compelled to pay claims incurred under its authority.[1] The case confirms Oklahoma's position among the small but growing number of states which have created a central state board of higher education empowered to allocate funds to the several institutions and have made commendable efforts to relieve the institutions from unseemly biennial battling in legislative halls and committee rooms.

CONSTRUING AN APPROPRIATION ACT

The University of Alabama purchased the Jefferson Hospital in Birmingham subject to an indebtedness of $1,200,000 to the Reconstruction Finance Corporation. Since an Alabama statute of 1945 appropriated the proceeds of the state income tax for that year "to be released upon the approval of the governor" for the payment of any debts of the state or any of its agencies or institutions, an injunction was sought by the state superintendent of education to prevent payment of the debt to the RFC. Among the numerous and far-fetched arguments were these: the act made an unconstitutional delegation of legislative power to the governor; it did not represent the legislative intent, because it was enacted in anticipation of an income tax amendment which was later defeated, and because a later act of the same session referred to the Jefferson Hospital debt as a "deferrable project." The court found no merit in any of the arguments, upheld the act, and refused to interfere with its execution.[2]

PARTICULAR EXPENDITURES UNDER APPROPRIATION ACTS

An Arizona appropriation act of 1945 for the state institutions of higher education expressly included "for payment of

1 *Board of Regents of University of Oklahoma et al.* v. *Childress, State Auditor, et al.* (Okla.), 170 P. 2d 1018 (1946).

2 *Norton* v. *Lusk et al.* (Ala.), 26 So. 2d 849 (1946).

assessments or membership fees in societies, associations and organizations; for travel to attend meetings, conferences and for other college purposes. . . ." Even in the face of this explicit authorization, the state auditor hesitated to certify claims of the board of regents of the university and state colleges for these very purposes.

The state auditor was erroneously influenced by an earlier court decision against payment by cities of dues in a municipal league when there was no statutory authority for such expenditures of public funds. In fact, however, there is a long judicial tradition in Arizona that the state auditor cannot interfere with the disbursement of funds which have passed to the control of the board of regents and which are obligated for a public purpose as evidenced by the 1923 case of *Fairfield* v. *W. J. Corbett Hardware Company*. After reviewing this history, the court concluded that the claims were obviously legitimate and gently admonished the auditor thus:

> If a claim shows on its face that it is for a public purpose and is properly itemized, accompanied by vouchers, is approved by the head of the department and there are still unappropriated funds for the payment of same, it is not her duty to investigate farther and she should approve the claim and issue the warrant.[3]

The same state auditor had to be again coerced by *mandamus* in a second case, to issue warrants in payment of claims incurred for the expenses of the inauguration of a new president of the University of Arizona. Items included were rental of academic costumes for delegates, luncheon and reception, photographers' services, programs, direction signs, announcements, invitations, information folders, and the use of a public address system. The court held that these expenses were for a public purpose, and that the auditor's duty in such circumstances is merely ministerial and not discretionary.

Chief Justice La Prade spoke at some length in quotable style:

[3] *Frohmiller* v. *Board of Regents of University and State Colleges* (Ariz.), 171 P. 2d 356 (1946).

Ceremony, it is true, is not a necessity; a new president could be seated with no more ceremony than attends the swearing in of a constable, but this overlooks the nature of an institution of higher learning, the character and needs of a large body of undergraduates and their professors; the loyalties inspired in them by their university; the value of ritual and symbolism in developing these loyalties in formative minds; the calling of attention to the unity of all the colleges and schools of the university and the centering of control of a vast educational plant with its multitude of diverse interests and aspirations in the president. The dignity of the office is enhanced by such ceremonies. A failure to avail the university of the opportunity to signalize the importance of this event in its life when the reins of control are transferred to a new president might more readily subject the board to a charge of laxity and indifference to the psychological values inherent in the occasion than of extravagance for providing for a ceremonious celebration of so important an event.

A peremptory writ of *mandamus* was issued to compel the auditor to act. One member of the court, Justice Phelps, dissented, solely on the ground that he did not regard *mandamus* as the proper remedy. He thought the auditor has a quasi-judicial duty, and that in a case of this type the holders of claims against the university should be relegated to the remedy at law—suit for breach of contract.[4]

CUSTODY AND USE OF NON-TAX FUNDS OF STATE INSTITUTIONS

There is a diversity of practice among the states as to the disposition of moneys coming into the possession of state institutions from nontax sources. Under one extreme these funds must go promptly into the state treasury, and not be available to the institution unless and until appropriated to it by the legislature. Another view is that such moneys properly remain in the custody of the institution itself, and may be expended at the discretion of its governing board for any of its legitimate purposes, without

[4] *Board of Regents of University and State Colleges v. Frohmiller*, 69 Ariz. 50, 208 P. 2d 833 (1949).

the intervention of the legislature or of any other state authority. This is the better theory. One of the states in which it is currently practiced is Arkansas, and an Arkansas decision of 1949 sustained the practice.

A taxpayer's suit was brought to enjoin the University of Arkansas and the several other state institutions from paying out any funds not appropriated by the legislature, and to require them to deposit all their receipts in the state treasury. Also it was sought specifically to enjoin the institutions from using their receipts from nontax sources to supplement the salaries of certain employees so as to exceed the maximum salaries specified in the current appropriation act. The trial court dismissed the case, and the supreme court of Arkansas affirmed the judgment, except as to the last point. Here it was held that the plaintiff was entitled to an injunction against the payment of salaries in excess of those provided for in the appropriation act, but that the injunction should not apply to the use of funds received from sources not controlled by the legislature, such as federal subventions, endowment income, current gifts, and student fees.

Two sections of the Arkansas Constitution of 1874 stipulate that no money shall go out of the state treasury except as appropriated by law; but there is no requirement that the funds at issue in this case shall go *into* the state treasury. The legislature could so prescribe, but it has not done so. This was the opinion of Justice McFaddin and the entire court except Chief Justice Griffin Smith, who dissented vigorously but on dubious reasoning. He could not believe that the framers of the constitution had *intended* to omit the deposit requirement.[5]

STATE AID TO DENOMINATIONAL INSTITUTIONS

New York's recent State Emergency Housing Act authorized allocations of state money to colleges and universities for additional student facilities, and under this act allotments were

[5] *Gipson* v. *Ingram et al.* (Ark.), 223 S.W. 2d 595 (1949).

made to several Catholic colleges in the state. A taxpayer in Buffalo, suing to enjoin the allocation of $128,000 to Canisius College, lost his case in the trial court and also in the appellate division by a vote of four to one of the judges.

The decision did not turn upon the actual issue of unconstitutionality of the act, however, because the complainant was barred by another New York statute which prevents the bringing of such a suit by an ordinary citizen and taxpayer and allows it to be brought only by a taxpayer who can allege and show that he is suffering a special and particular grievance as a result of the act he challenges.[6]

[6] Decision of the New York Appellate Division, Third Department, as reported in the New York *Times*, March 24, 1948.

CHAPTER X

EXEMPTION FROM PROPERTY TAXES

THE exemption of institutional property of various kinds from state and local property taxation concerns colleges and universities of all types; but cases involving state or municipal institutions reach the higher courts only relatively rarely. A decision regarding the University of Michigan has been noted in Chapter VII, and a case involving an accessory educational corporation at the University of Wisconsin appears in the final chapter of this volume. The present chapter and the four chapters immediately following it deal almost wholly with cases touching privately controlled institutions.

Recent decisions as to the exemption of specific types of college and university property, such as athletic plants and housing for faculty members, appear here; as do also cases touching other property held under varying circumstances and conditions, including real property devoted solely to income-producing purposes.

HOUSING FOR FACULTY MEMBERS

In 1946 New Jersey denied the claims of the city of Hoboken regarding the taxability of numerous and varied parts of the physical plant of Stevens Institute of Technology.[1] In 1947 this decision was slightly modified, to the extent that four dwelling houses owned by the institute and rented to faculty members must be held taxable unless and until evidence is offered as to whether the rentals are such as to return no profit to the insti-

[1] *City of Hoboken v. Division of Tax Appeals, Department of Taxation and Finance, et al.* (N.J. Sup.), 49 A. 2d 587 (1946).

tute. This decision was supported by nine of the justices, as against four who voted for affirmance of the lower court judgment of complete exemption. The exemption statute contains a proviso that "the buildings . . . are not conducted for profit." [2]

A Vermont decision of 1949 is also adverse to the exemption of a particular building used for faculty housing. A privately controlled junior college acquired a large residence in 1945, located about 200 yards from the campus, and used it to house eight members of the faculty, who took salary deductions of $400 a year for room and board or $160 for room only. The trial court adjudged the house exempt, relying chiefly on a section of the institutional charter (a special legislative act of 1834) which declared "all necessary buildings of the institution . . . shall be exempt from taxation." But the supreme court of Vermont pointed out that another section of the charter specifically reserved to the state the right of amendment or repeal. The house would be exempt, thought the court, under Section 590 of the *Public Laws,* which is a general exemption of college property not rented for commercial purposes; but both this section and the exemption section of the special act of 1834 were modified by Section 1 of No. 12 of the *Acts of 1941,* which stipulates that

> any real property acquired after passage of this bill by any college . . . such as would be exempt from taxation under the provisions of section 590 of the *Public Laws* . . . shall be set to such institution in the grand list of the town or city . . . and taxed; *provided,* however, that the voters of any town or city may at any legal meeting thereof vote to exempt such property from taxation. . . .

The opinion of the court contains a lengthy and scholarly review of the earlier New England decisions on the taxability of faculty and student housing.[3]

A trial court decision in New York is unequivocally favorable

[2] *City of Hoboken* v. *Division of Tax Appeals, Dept. of Taxation and Finance* (N.J.L.), 55 A. 2d 290 (1947).

[3] *Troy Conference Academy and Green Mountain Junior College* v. *Town of Poultney et al.* (Vt.), 66 A. 2d 2 (1949).

to the exemption of faculty housing owned by an educational institution. The Thomas G. Clarkson Memorial College of Technology offers courses in engineering, chemistry, and business administration. Located in Potsdam, Lawrence County, New York, it found great expansion of its facilities necessary in recent years, and accordingly bought several houses in Potsdam and also opened a branch institution at Malone in Franklin County. The litigated issue concerned the taxation of six houses in Potsdam which had been purchased and used largely for housing students in 1946, but during the following year gradually were converted largely to the housing of faculty members.

This raised the ancient issue of taxing professors' houses owned by a college and brought forth some clear-cut comment from the judge of the local supreme court. First noting that the physical location of the houses is immaterial if they are part of an integrated and articulated educational system operated by the college, he then proceeded to brush aside any alleged distinction from an educational viewpoint, between housing for students and housing for faculty members.

> I can find no justification for making a distinction between a dormitory, either simple or elaborate, in which students may room at a stated rental, or a dining hall, in which they may buy their meals, on the one hand, and, on the other, a dwelling or an apartment in which one of their teachers may live, either alone or in common with his family, eating, sleeping and, of course, performing necessary out-of-class tasks, even though, in it, as a private residence, he might choose to assert his rights of castle.

The judge thought judicial sanction ought to be given to the administrative policy of regarding faculty residences as exempt from taxation when owned by a tax-exempt educational institution for that purpose. The old distinctions as to payment of rentals as against free rent as a part of compensation, so carefully made in early Massachusetts decisions, he regarded as not properly material, because they go to the form rather than the substance of the relationship and are obviously subject to manipulation. Accordingly, all the houses in dispute were stricken from the tax rolls except one which was leased to an occupant not connected with the college in any capacity, under a condition in the lease that if she kept any roomers or boarders, they must be students or faculty members of the college.[4]

ATHLETIC PLANTS IN NEW JERSEY

Rutgers University's 138 acres of athletic fields and stadium across the Raritan River are not exempt from taxation, said a New Jersey trial court, nor is the assessed valuation of the million-dollar stadium excessive when fixed at $60,000, as it was for the year 1942. A statute exempts college buildings and a five-acre curtilage "actually used for colleges." Readily conceding that physical education is a proper subject of instruction, Judge Colie questioned the necessity of "stands to accommodate 20,000 spectators when the enrollment of the university is under 1,700," and concluded that the primary use of the stadium was something other than for the physical education of college students.[5]

Two athletic fields at Stevens Institute of Technology are adjudged properly exempt under the same statute, however, because they contain no permanent stands for paying spectators and are apparently actually used as playing-fields and not as arenas for huge public exhibitions. The city of Hoboken also sought unsuccessfully to tax certain dormitories, dining halls, residences for the president and faculty members, a gymnasium, and a "towing tank research laboratory" built during the war for research related to the war effort. Regarding the latter, the court emphatically enunciated that research is a college function no less than instruction.[6]

[4] *Application of Thomas G. Clarkson Memorial College of Technology* (Misc.), 77 N.Y.S. 2d 182 (1948).

[5] *Trustees of Rutgers University* v. *Piscataway Twp. in Middlesex County et al.* (N.J. Sup.), 46 A. 2d 56 (1946).

[6] *City of Hoboken* v. *Division of Tax Appeals, Department of Taxation and Finance et al.* (N.J. Sup.), 49 A. 2d 587 (1946). Modified as to four houses rented to faculty members, in *Same* (N.J.L.), 55 A. 2d 290 (1947), cited in Footnote 2 of this chapter.

SITE OF RESEARCH PLANT INVOLVED IN CONTRACT BETWEEN UNIVERSITY AND FEDERAL GOVERNMENT

A Maryland decision of 1946 was made necessary on account of the purchase by Johns Hopkins University of 40 acres near Washington and the erection of a research plant on the site. When the Maryland county in which the site is located sought to tax the land against the university as record owner, it was found that under the terms of the contract between the federal government and the university, the federal government was the equitable owner of the real beneficial interest in the land, and it was accordingly not taxable because the states and their agencies do not tax federal property. The question of research as tax-exempt use was not raised.[7]

REAL PROPERTY HELD AS INVESTMENT

Howard University in the District of Columbia owns various dwellings, apartments, and stores in the vicinity of its campus, and rents them. Their aggregate assessed value is about three quarters of a million dollars. A small fraction of this property is carried as endowment and its income used for current operating expenses; but the bulk of it is held as assets under the Twenty-Year Extension Plan of 1929, which contemplates the ultimate accumulation of $15,000,000 to be expended for the erection of university buildings. The university charter is an act of Congress of 1867, and an amendment of 1882 exempts its property from taxation "only so long as such property shall be used only for the purposes set forth. . . ." These purposes are epitomized as "the education of youth." Such an exemption clause, decided the Court of Appeals for the District of Columbia, must be construed as not exempting the real estate used merely for income-producing purposes and would be so construed in a majority, though not all, of the states. Quoting a Nebraska decision under a somewhat similar statute, "The law

[7] *Johns Hopkins University* v. *Board of County Commissioners of Montgomery County et al.* (Md.), 45 A. 2d 747 (1946).

looks to the property as it finds it in use, and not to what is done with its accumulations." [8]

A section of the South Carolina Constitution contains a self-executing exemption from taxation of college property, but specifies that such property shall not be exempt unless it is occupied by the college. A depression-born statute of 1936 purported to exempt for five years property acquired for foreclosure if the income from it was not sufficient to pay the taxes. Wofford College and Converse College had several parcels of real property in Spartanburg which were within the definition of the statute from 1936 to 1943; but a state supreme court decision of 1942 declared the statute unconstitutional, and subsequently the property was assessed and taxed. In a second suit Wofford College sought to maintain the exemption for the years 1936 to 1942, but the decision was adverse, on the simple principle that tax abatements under authority of a statute later held unconstitutional are void.[9]

BUILDINGS ERECTED BY A LONG-TERM COMMERCIAL LESSEE

An interesting question is presented when property is owned by a nonprofit educational corporation but is in the hands of a long-term lessee for commercial uses. Is it taxable against the lessee as his own property? Generally yes, either on the theory that a long-term lease is the practical equivalent of a sale, or on other grounds, as in the case wherein the Southern Baptist Theological Seminary moved to a roomier location and leased its abandoned downtown Louisville site to a commercial corporation for 99 years, stipulating that any buildings erected by the lessee would become the property of the seminary "as erected." Despite this stipulation, the court decided that the Greyhound Bus Station and a large garage erected on the site

[8] *Howard University* v. *District of Columbia* (U.S.C.A. for D.C.), 155 F. 2d 18 (1946).

[9] *Trustees of Wofford College* v. *Burnett* (S.C.), 39 S.E. 2d 155 (1946).

were taxable against the lessee. Taxing the land itself was not at issue. Said the court:

It can readily be foreseen that tax-exempt organizations might be extensively used by commercial organizations to evade payment of taxes on real estate improvements through the medium of long-term leases, if we should deny the right of a taxing authority to make separate assessments of buildings and of lands in cases of this kind.[10]

EDUCATIONAL PLANT LEASED FROM A NON-CHARITABLE CORPORATION

In most jurisdictions, but not in all, property of a private proprietor is generally not exempt from taxation, even while leased and used for educational purposes by a nonprofit agency, especially if the rental paid is more than nominal. Thus, where an improved park property was owned by a no-dividend noncharitable stock corporation and leased to the International Pentecostal Assemblies (a charitable corporation which used it as a theological school for the training of ministers and missionaries and obligated itself for annual rentals equivalent to about $1,000 a year), the Wyoming supreme court unanimously held that the property continued taxable against the noncharitable owner.[11]

PARK HELD BY COLLEGE IN TRUST FOR THE PUBLIC

A Vermont statute makes college-owned timberlands taxable; but the extensive wooded park administered by Middlebury College is not held by the college as owner, but as trustee for the public under the will of the donor who created the trust. In asserting a right to tax the property, the town of Hancock contended that the college had violated the trust by unauthorized

[10] *Broadway and Fourth Avenue Realty Company* v. *City of Louisville* (Ky.), 197 S.W. 2d 238 (1946).

[11] *Commissioners of Cambria Park* v. *Board of County Commissioners of Weston County et al.* (Wyo.), 174 P. 2d 402 (1946).

cutting and selling of timber; but the college successfully countered that it had cut and removed only disease-infested trees, in order to save the forest from destruction. Moreover, said the court, "unwarranted cutting and sale of timber . . . could not prejudice the trust estate or transform a public use into a private use, any more than a similar cutting and sale by a trespasser. . . ." In other words maladministration by a trustee does not affect the nature of a trust; and a court will intervene to correct the maladministration, even by removing the trustee and appointing another, if necessary. Middlebury College is not the owner of the beneficial interest in this instance, because proceeds from the park are applied only to park improvements, such as roads, ski trails, stocks of trout for the lake, and shelters for hikers. These facilities are open to the general public, either free or at nominal fees.[12]

[12] *President and Fellows of Middlebury College* v. *Town of Hancock* (Vt.), 55 A. 2d 194 (1947).

CHAPTER XI

SOME TESTS OF EXEMPTION FROM PROPERTY TAXES UNDER VARIOUS STATE STATUTES

THE most common test of property tax exemption is that of ownership and use for nonprofit charitable purposes. This is not, however, the test in all states. The wording of the exemption clauses of the constitutions and statutes varies greatly, as do also the facts of the cases to which they apply. Some recent decisions emphasizing the tests of exemption, and disclosing certain trends as well as some oddities, compose this chapter.

AN INCIPIENT TREND IN OHIO?

Ohio has long had two statutes exempting (1) property used exclusively for public worship, and (2) property of a "public college or academy or a public institution on learning not used with a view to profit." A series of harsh decisions under these statutes has for a time resulted in taxing the property of certain nonprofit theological seminaries. A leading case was *Bloch v. Board of Tax Appeals* (1945), digested at page 61 in *The Colleges and the Courts, 1941–45*. That decision was reaffirmed in 1947 in a second action involving the same Orthodox Jewish theological school. Here, in the language of Justice Hart of the Ohio supreme court, the doctrine of the decision is much clearer than in the earlier case:

A school organized and operated by a religious denomination for the sole purpose of training men to assume ministerial positions in such denomination, and which provides no educational opportunities to the public generally, is essentially a private institution, and a building housing such a school is not exempt from taxation as being a public school or public institution of learning, or property used exclusively for a charitable purpose.[1]

The same doctrine was adhered to in a subsequent case in which a lot and two-story brick building in Cleveland, used exclusively for the housing and training of newly ordained priests of a Roman Catholic order for missionary work among the Negroes of the city, were held to be taxable since the year 1937, when the property was put on the tax duplicate. Residents of the house were the priest in charge and seven students, all ordained priests. The court followed and approved its decisions in the *Bloch* and *Telshe* cases.[2]

In 1949 the Ohio supreme court found itself divided in another and somewhat similar case. Here an institution affiliated with the Society of Friends, offering a four-year course for the degree of Bachelor of Theology, a four-year course for the degree of Bachelor of Sacred Music, and a two-year junior college course in liberal arts, was contending for the exemption of its physical plant, a chief focus of dispute being a lot of 7,000 square feet containing a three-story stone dormitory for girls. Originally exemption had been denied on the ground that the school was open only to adherents of the Christian religion in some form, and not to the public generally; but thereafter the religious qualification was deleted, so that the following statement could be made: "The college is open to the public, to all graduates of an accredited high school regardless of race, color or religion, subject only to the ability of the college to take care of its applicants. Among the students are some who have indicated no denominational affiliation."

By the narrow vote of four justices against three, the court reversed the ruling of the Board of Tax Appeals which had de-

1 *American Committee of Rabbinical College of Telshe* v. *Board of Tax Appeals*, 148 Ohio St. 654, 76 N.E. 2d 719 (1947).

2 *Society of Precious Blood* v. *Board of Tax Appeals*, 149 Ohio St. 62, 77 N.E. 2d 459 (1948), affirming *Application of Society of Precious Blood* (Ohio B.T.A.), 71 N.E. 2d 278 (1947).

nied the exemption. In the majority were Justices Hart, Stewart, Turner, and Taft. In a specially concurring opinion, Justice Taft argued cogently that an institution can be "used exclusively for charitable purposes" even though it restricts admission to followers of some lawful religion. He cast doubt upon the correctness of the decisions in the *Bloch, Telshe,* and *Precious Blood* cases, believing them to be based on a decision prior to the constitutional revision of 1912 (which amended the constitutional exemption provisions slightly and was followed by implementing legislation). In this position Justice Stewart concurred.

The dissenting minority consisted of Chief Justice Weygandt and Justices Matthias and Zimmerman. Approving the *Bloch* and *Telshe* decisions, they asserted that an institution can not be "used exclusively for charitable purposes" unless it is open to the public generally; and that a dormitory in which all residents pay rent is *ipso facto* not a charitable institution.[3] Neither of these propositions commends itself. The outspoken revolt of Justices Taft and Stewart may presage a retreat from the harsh precedents which have seemed puzzling and difficult to support.

EXCLUSIVE USE FOR EXEMPT PURPOSES

In Rhode Island a Roman Catholic order owning a building used as a residence for nuns and occasional guests who came for religious activities, and for instruction of children of the parish, sought its exemption on the ground that its *primary* use was religious. Denying the application and holding the building taxable, the Rhode Island supreme court declared that the test is *exclusive* religious use, and that a building used in part as a residence, even of a priest, can not be said to be used exclusively for religious purposes.[4]

[3] *Cleveland Bible College* v. *Board of Tax Appeals,* 151 Ohio St. 258, 85 N.E. 2d 284 (1949).

[4] *Sisterhood of Holy Nativity* v. *Tax Assessors of City of Newport* (R.I.), 57 A. 2d 184 (1948).

In Texas, the exemption of property educationally used is dependent solely on its being "used exclusively and owned by persons or associations of persons for school purposes," and follows this principle without distinction between nonprofit and proprietary institutions. A 1950 case illustrates the point. A proprietary post-high school three-year school of design (interior decorating, costume design, commercial art, merchandising display) in Houston, owned and operated by a family partnership, sought exemption of its plant, consisting of a lot with a building at each end—the one building being used wholly for the purposes of the school, and the other being used partly for those purposes and partly as a residence for the family of proprietors. In these circumstances the city was enjoined from carrying the first building on the tax rolls, but left free to tax the second building. The Court of Civil Appeals was careful to make clear that in this case the residence of the proprietors in a part of the school plant appeared to be merely a matter of convenience, and not essential to the purposes of the school, as is sometimes the case where the managers of a boarding school reside in the school building because that is necessary for properly supervising the good order, safety, and morals of the students out of school hours.

When the case reached the supreme court of Texas, that tribunal affirmed the judgment as to the year 1947, but held that the injunction against carrying the indicated building on the tax rolls must be limited to that year, because in 1948 and 1949 the record showed that the building was owned exclusively by the husband and wife, but the school was operated during those two years by a partnership composed of the husband, the wife, and their adult daughter; thus the operators were not identical with the owners, and that circumstance, said the court, destroyed the exemption under the wording of the exemption statute. In the course of the opinion Chief Justice Hickman took occasion to explain the historical origin of the principle that proprietary institutions are intended to be exempt from taxation if they come within the wording of the statute.[5]

DISTINCTION BETWEEN GENERAL AND VOCATIONAL EDUCATIONAL USES IN MICHIGAN

A business school in Detroit, although it had been chartered as a nonprofit corporation in 1941, was held liable for approximately $800 in personal property taxes for the years 1942–46, because, in the words of Justice Sharpe of the Michigan supreme court, "It is a specialized school operated for the purpose of training its students into specialized fields of employment. It is not such a school or college as is entitled to tax exemption." The court did not intimate any doubt of the *bona fide* nonprofit character of the school, but based its decision entirely upon Michigan precedents holding institutions of *general* or *academic* or *preparatory* education exempt from taxation, but schools of *specialized* or *vocational* or *terminal* education taxable. Thus it cited a Michigan decision of 1920 wherein a proprietary academic preparatory school was declared exempt, and a decision of 1911 in which a nonprofit incorporated business college was held taxable.[6]

[5] *Smith et al.* v. *Feather et ux.* (Tex.), 234 S.W. 2d 418 (1950), reforming and affirming *Same* (Tex. Civ. App.), 229 S.W. 417 (1950).

[6] *City of Detroit et al.* v. *Detroit Commercial College*, 322 Mich. 142, 33 N.W. 2d 737 (1948).

CHAPTER XII

PROPERTY TAX EXEMPTION OF VARIOUS TYPES OF INSTITUTIONS

COLLEGES and universities constitute only one of many varieties of institutions and organizations in our pluralistic society which are generally nonprofit and charitable in character and perform services traditionally embraced in the category of "charities." In the classic legal definition of charity, education is one of four great types of service; even within this smaller sphere, institutions of higher education share the field with numerous other types of agencies, such as private schools of less than college level, art galleries, symphony orchestras, libraries, professional and scientific societies, and many others. Decisions regarding these other types of educational agencies have relevance at this point.

PRIVATE SCHOOLS TRANSMUTED FROM PROPRIETARY STATUS

Several cases involving the taxation of schools originally proprietary but later metamorphosed into nonprofit charitable corporations have been digested in the predecessors of this volume. Two more such cases are now to be added.

In Montclair, New Jersey, a private preparatory school for girls (admitting also a few boys in the lower grades) was founded in 1906 and operated by two women proprietors until it was incorporated as a nonprofit institution in 1941. The corporation then leased the plant from the proprietors, and in 1943 it purchased the plant from them for $50,000, chiefly on credit, and agreed to pay interest at the rate of 5 percent on the loan.

In that year there was a small net excess of income over expenditures. Salaries of employees were fixed at the discretion of the headmistress. Influenced by the fact that the reorganization did not involve any increase in endowment funds or any substantial augmentation of charitable gifts, but was merely a sale of the property to the new corporation, the Department of Taxation ordered the property restored to the tax rolls for the years 1944, 1945, and 1946, at the petition of the town of Montclair.[1]

In a Pennsylvania case the school in question was a business corporation until 1929, when its venerable headmistress had it reorganized to become a charitable corporation. She continued as headmistress at an annual salary of $20,000, and in 1947 she was receiving $8,000 a year and the use of a house. In 1945 she gave the school 35 acres of real estate, valued at $70,000 and assessed at $40,000. This brought the total holdings of the school up to 82 acres, assessed at over $800,000, and stimulated the township in which it is located to question the tax exemption of the whole. It alleged that the exemption created a hardship for the local governmental unit; and that the nonprofit organization of the school was primarily for the purpose of avoiding taxation. Unimpressed by these arguments, the trial court held that the entire property is exempt. Says the syllabus:

> A private school existing as a nonprofit corporation for the education of young women, charging substantial tuition, having an endowment, granting scholarships, open to any young woman meeting the educational standards without restriction as to race, creed, or similar limitation, . . . is exempt from taxation under Article IX, Section 1, of the State Constitution, and the act of May 3, 1943, *Public Law 158*.[2]

PLANTS OF INDEPENDENT RESEARCH CORPORATIONS

Two decisions, in Ohio and New Jersey respectively, are adverse to the exemption of nonprofit research institutes, each of

[1] *Town of Montclair* v. *Kimberly School* (N.J. Department of Taxation), 51 A. 2d 228 (1947).

[2] *Township of Abingdon et al.* v. *Ogontz School* (Pa. Com. Pl.), 64 Montg. 285 (1947).

which is located near a large university but in no sense subsidiary to it.

The Ohio supreme court decided that the large and valuable plant and equipment of the Battelle Memorial Institute in Columbus, an endowed charitable institution for scientific research, must be taxed because a major portion of the annual income of the institution comes from research projects executed under contracts with private industrial firms which receive exclusive rights to the results and at least temporarily withhold the benefits from the general public. The picture is not materially affected by the fact that the institute provides a number of fellowships for needy graduate students at near-by Ohio State University.[3]

Likewise, the Textile Research Institute, operating a research laboratory near Princeton University, must pay taxes to the state of New Jersey on the site and buildings on two grounds: (1) it is incorporated in the state of New York and is a "foreign corporation" not covered by the New Jersey statute exempting "all buildings actually and exclusively used in the work of associations and corporations organized exclusively for the moral and mental improvement of men, women and children," and (2) its purpose was primarily to benefit the textile industry, and "Neither Princeton University nor any other college or university has any jurisdiction over it." The issue was unaffected by the fact that the Institute subsidizes fellowships in the graduate school at Princeton.[4]

PROPERTY OF AGRICULTURAL SOCIETY

A Massachusetts statute specifically exempts "real and personal estate of incorporated agricultural societies and the portions of real estate and buildings of incorporated horticultural societies used for their offices, libraries, and exhibitions." An agricultural society owning a brick-and-steel coliseum and ap-

[3] *Battelle Memorial Institute* v. *Dunn* (Ohio St.), 73 N.E. 2d 88 (1947).

[4] *Textile Research Institute* v. *Princeton Township* (N.J. Dept. of Taxation and Finance, Division of Tax Appeals), 50 A. 2d 829 (1946).

purtenant grounds in West Springfield regularly conducts therein an agricultural fair during the third week of September, and occasional other activities connected with the advancement of agriculture at other times. When not in use for agricultural purposes, the premises have been leased for a part of each year since 1925, except the war years, for the promotion of sporting events; and in 1946 they were leased for a series of seven-month terms for the conduct of ice hockey games. All revenue of the agricultural society from whatever source is used for the conduct of its business, the reduction of indebtedness incurred in the acquisition of the real estate, and the construction of buildings.

The property is held to be exempt. Said Justice Wilkins, for the whole court:

> The power to lease property to make it produce income is an incident of ownership. . . . Such a prudent use of the building is not *ultra vires*. . . . It is common knowledge that the main use of the real estate of agricultural societies is as a site for a seasonal fair. The encouragement to agriculture would be slight indeed if tax exemption, so broadly expressed, be held to be conditional upon such property remaining idle or unprofitable at all times when not needed for direct agricultural pursuits.[5]

ART GALLERY IN NEW YORK

Under New York statutes, property of a tax-exempt educational corporation is not exempt where it is held as an investment, even though the income be used for the nonprofit corporate purpose. The test of exemption is *both* ownership and *exclusive* use for charitable purposes. The Frick Art Gallery, housed at Nos. 1 and 3 East Seventieth Street in New York City, purchased the premises at No. 7 for use in expanding its facilities; but decided to postpone demolition and construction, and in the meantime to rent the property. Accordingly it was leased at a rental of $12,000 a year to the Asia Institute, another non-

[5] *Assessors of West Springfield* v. *Eastern States Exposition* (Mass.), 93 N.E. 2d 462 (1950).

profit educational corporation chartered by the Board of Regents of the University of the State of New York. In this situation the property was taxable, though owned by the exempt corporation and rented by another. If either corporation had *owned and used* the premises, it would have been exempt.[6]

GYMNASTIC ASSOCIATION

In 1904, in the noted case of *German Gymnastic Association* v. *Louisville,* the plant of that organization was declared exempt from taxation as an educational institution, on the basis, in part, of a schedule of organized class instruction in literary subjects one day each week. As noted at pages 67 and 68 in *The Colleges and the Courts, 1941–45,* the same court forty years later concluded that this decision should be overruled, in the 1945 case of *Kesselring* v. *Bonnycastle Club.* When, however, the city sought to collect taxes for the years 1942–46, and was sustained by the trial court, the Court of Appeals in 1948 agreed that the Gymnastic Association is no longer classified as an educational institution, and that the decision of 1904 is not *res judicata* so as to bar all future taxation; but, said the court, although the 1945 decision declared that the 1904 decision should be overruled, it did not expressly and effectively overrule it. Hence the judgment of the lower court holding the Gymnastic Association taxable from 1942 to 1946 was reversed; but the judgment that the association is taxable in the future was affirmed, to be effective upon the effective date of the Court of Appeals decision of 1948.[7]

[6] *People ex rel. Frick Collection* v. *Chambers et al., Tax Commission of City of New York* (Misc.), 91 N.Y.S. 2d 515 (1949).

[7] *German Gymnastic Association of Louisville* v. *City of Louisville,* 306 Ky. 810, 209 S.W. 2d 75 (1948).

CHAPTER XIII

STATE TAXES OTHER THAN PROPERTY TAXES

STATE statutes providing for succession taxes on the transfer of inheritances, gifts, or estates, usually afford exemptions for transfers to charitable or educational institutions, and hence give rise to some litigation involving colleges and universities. Cases involving other types of state taxes also occasionally reach the higher courts.

STATE INHERITANCE TAXES

A Kentucky testator's will, after making specific bequests to certain relatives and leaving a portion of the estate undevised, then gave the residuary part to a nephew for life, and at his death to the University of Louisville. On behalf of the several legatees it was contended that both the state inheritance tax and the federal estate tax should be paid out of the undevised property. Neither branch of this contention could be sustained. As to the federal estate tax, the most elementary rule is that it must be levied on the whole estate, less deductible exemptions. As to the state inheritance tax, its incidence is upon each separate legacy as a whole. In the instance of the bequest to the nephew with deferred remainder to the university, this would result in all or part of the tax being borne by the university; but the court pointed out that "When the remainder goes to a corporation exempt from taxation, Kentucky Revised Statutes 140. 110 provides a method of recovery or refunding." [1]

[1] *Louisville Trust Company* v. *Walter et al.*, 306 Ky. 756, 207 S.W. 2d 328 (1948).

RECOMPUTATION OF TAX ON CHARITABLE BEQUEST AFFECTED BY CONTINGENCY

A section, enacted in 1935, of the Illinois inheritance tax statute provides

> where rights of beneficiaries are dependent upon contingencies whereby they may be wholly or in part created, defeated, extended or abridged, a tax shall be imposed at the highest rate which on the happening of any of the contingencies, would be possible; *provided,* that on the happening of any contingency whereby the property goes to a tax-exempt body, such shall be entitled to reassessment and refund.

Thus when a wealthy Chicagoan bequeathed a large residue of his $9,000,000 estate to a tax-exempt organization known as the Arboretum Trust, subject to contingencies such that the amount of the legacy to the Arboretum Trust was contingent upon the longevity of the donor's widow, the statute was applied.

The will directed that the entire income of this legacy should be accumulated for two years. Thereafter for eight years, one half of the income should be added to the corpus, and one half paid to the decedent's widow, son, and daughter. At the end of the ten-year period the whole corpus should go to these three persons, if living; but if the widow were deceased within that period, thereafter one half of her share of income and corpus should be disposed of as she might have appointed, and one half to the Arboretum Trust. At the testator's death the widow's interest was worth more than $3,000,000, and an inheritance tax of $392,000 was paid, on the assumption that she would survive the ten-year period. She died within the period, and "by reason of her death prior to the expiration of the ten-year period, . . . the tax should have been $31,000." Accordingly the Arboretum Trust asked for a reassessment and refund of approximately $361,000, and the petition was granted.[2]

[2] *In re Morton's Estate* (Ill.), 72 N.E. 2d 809 (1947).

DEFINING "EDUCATIONAL" UNDER THE NEW JERSEY INHERITANCE TAX STATUTES

New Jersey statutes provide total exemption for "educational institutions," but only partial exemption for other "benevolent and charitable organizations." How would the nonprofit corporation maintaining the De Wint House in Rockland County, New York, as a historical museum, be classified? A New Jersey intermediate court has recently held that "eduational" must be equated with "colleges, schools, academies, or seminaries" in which there is the daily teacher-student relationship. Hence a bequest to the De Wint House is entitled only to the partial exemption. The court took the narrow view that, although concededly serving important educational purposes, "libraries and museums devoted to public use are not strictly places of instruction such as schools." [3] The whole tendency of the times is toward acceptance of a broader interpretation of the adjective "educational."

WHEN THE STATUTE DOES NOT EXEMPT THE LEGATEE

The residual estate, valued at $2,471,758.49, of a resident of Cook County, Illinois, was bequeathed to the Regents of the University of Wisconsin. The state of Illinois collected an inheritance tax of $714,097.55, which was protested on the ground that the words of the statute, "A tax is hereby imposed upon the transfer . . . to persons, institutions or corporations, not hereinafter exempted," do not embrace an agency of a sovereign state such as Wisconsin. It was also argued that under the United States Constitution, one state can not tax the property of another. These arguments were erroneous. It was long ago established that an inheritance tax is not a tax levied on property,

[3] *Tappan Washington Memorial Corporation* v. *Margetts*, 9 N.J. Super. 212, 75 A. 2d 823 (1950).

but upon the privilege of receiving a transfer of property; that the right of ownership of the amount of the tax vests in the taxing jurisdiction *before* the legacy passes to the legatee; hence there is no question of one jurisdiction taxing property of another.[4] On behalf of the legatee in this case, no contention was made that it was exempt under the Illinois statute; the argument rested on the unsupportable proposition that the statute did not embrace or apply to this legatee at all. Accordingly judgment in favor of the state of Illinois was affirmed.[5]

In the California case of *Fleming's Estate,* discussed in Chapter IV, a fund was given to a trustee bank to be administered to provide scholarships for recipients not necessarily residents of California; the gift was subject to the California inheritance tax, because under the exemption clause of 1917 such a gift must be either to a charitable corporation within the state, or limited to use within the state. The court thought this view of the case could not be affected by the fact that an amendment of 1929 provided for extending the exemption by reciprocity with other states enacting reciprocal exemptions, and that another amendment of 1939 made the exemption cover corporations chartered by the national government, in order to remove the California tax from national charitable organizations such as the American National Red Cross.[6]

GIFTS IN CONTEMPLATION OF DEATH

Hand in hand with inheritance tax laws go statutes taxing gifts *inter vivos* under circumstances demonstrating that they are made in contemplation of the early death of the donor and in lieu of a testamentary disposition. New Jersey has such a statute, and the state taxing authority ruled that the annual

[4] The classic case of *United States* v. *Perkins,* 163 U.S. 625, 16 S. Ct. 1073, 41 L. Ed. 287 (1896).

[5] *Board of Regents of University of Wisconsin* v. *State,* 404 Ill. 193, 88 N.E. 2d 489 (1949).

[6] *In re Fleming's Estate: Kuchel, Controller,* v. *First National Trust and Savings Bank of San Diego* (Cal.), 190 P. 2d 611 (1948); reversing *Same* (Cal. App.), 183 P. 2d 295 (1947).

gifts, aggregating nearly $3,000,000, by David B. Mills to the Davella Mills Foundation, from 1935 to his death in 1944 at the age of 86, were taxable. This ruling was overturned in the courts, upon evidence that the donor had continuously made various and large charitable gifts since 1908, and that he had created the donee foundation only after the death of his wife had deprived him of her services as advisory manager of his charities. Although he was aged 77 when he created the foundation, he was in excellent health, and actually lived nine years thereafter. His estate at death was worth more than $3,500,000—an amount greatly in excess of the total of his previous gifts to the foundation. All these facts were taken to indicate that the motive of the gifts was not to use them in lieu of a testamentary disposition, especially since the gifts were immediate and complete; and consequently they were not taxable as gifts in contemplation of death.[7]

The same case involved the valuation for inheritance tax purposes of 53,000 shares of General Motors stock bequeathed to the foundation in the will of Mr. Mills. On this point it was held these shares were properly assessed at 53,000 times the market value of one share, and not at a reduced value by application of the so-called "blockage" rule recognized by some federal courts in the past.

THE NEW YORK ESTATE TAX

The will of a New York testator disposed of a large estate by making a number of specific bequests of personality, devising to the testator's wife a life interest in certain real property which would go to Fordham University at her death, and directing that the transfer taxes be paid out of the residuary estate. It was found that this latter mandate would fall short of paying the taxes by some $3,000,000, and the court was faced with the necessity of determining "the order of abatement of specific devises

[7] *Montclair Trust Company et al. v. Zink, Commissioner of Taxation and Finance*, 141 N.J. Eq. 401, 57 A. 2d 372 (1948).

and bequests in order to pay such taxes." A fact of overriding significance was that the devise to the wife and Fordham University was made pursuant to an *ante-nuptial agreement* made in 1938 and modified in 1944, whereby both the wife and Fordham University became *creditors of the estate*, and property receivable by them as creditors would not be subject to any portion of the burden of the estate taxes. Moreover, the legacy to the university would be exempt for the additional reason that the legatee is a tax-exempt charitable corporation. Hence, to pay the estate taxes, first the residuary estate must be exhausted, and then resort must be had to the specific bequests of personalty.[8]

A New York resident died in 1944, bequeathing his residuary estate to his sister for life and then to the Hotchkiss School in Connecticut, of which the decedent was Headmaster Emeritus. The actuarily computed value of the remainder to pass to the Hotchkiss School would have been $63,619.14, had not the will contained this clause: "Should the welfare of my sister . . . require help in excess of the income available, I expressly authorize my trustees in their sole discretion to use a portion of the principal for such beneficiary." This raised a perennial question which has frequently been considered by federal courts in federal estate tax cases. Surrogate Griffiths lengthily reviewed the two lines of federal decisions on the point, and concluded by following the liberal doctrine of the *Ithaca Trust Company* case (1929).[9] "Welfare," thought he, connotes a material state whose requisites are calculable, and it is to be distinguished from "happiness" (a word sometimes used in clauses of this kind, but not here), which imports a state of mind. Therefore he concluded that a deduction of the amount of the gift to the Hotchkiss School was possible, but postponed determination of the amount of the deduction, pending receipt of evidence as to the financial resources of the sister and "other relevant facts." [10]

8 *In re Patterson's Will; Application of Townley, et al.* (N.Y. Sur.), 73 N.Y.S. 2d 433 (1947).

9 Mentioned and cited in the next chapter.

10 *In re Buell's Estate* (N.Y. Sur.), 66 N.Y.S. 2d 180 (1946).

UNEMPLOYMENT COMPENSATION TAX

The state unemployment compensation tax is still in the period of judicial testing of its application to professional societies. For example, is the American Medical Association "a society organized and operated exclusively for charitable, scientific, or educational purposes, no part of the net earnings of which inures to the benefit of any private shareholder or individual?" The Illinois supreme court thinks not, and finds a substantial part of its activities contribute in nowise to the exempted purposes and do not comply with the exemption features of the statute. A substantial portion of its income goes to further and protect private economic benefits to its members, and many of its activities and publications promote objects essentially similar to those of trade associations, labor unions, or retail merchants' associations, says the court.[11]

The Idaho unemployment compensation tax case of the *Gem State Academy Bakery* involved the status of certain nonstudent employees of a bakery operated by a nonprofit Seventh Day Adventist academy, the bakery being a part of the school's vocational education program, but also serving the general public in the vicinity commercially. Seven truck drivers employed on a commission basis to sell and deliver bakery products to the general public were held to be within the purview of the state unemployment compensation law, as was also the manager of the bakery to the extent of the one half of his salary which was chargeable to the commercial side of the bakery. This was the decision of the trial court. At first it was reversed by the supreme court of Idaho, in an opinion by Justice Taylor with Chief Justice Holden and Justice Keeton concurring, in which they concluded that since the church corporation owning the academy and the bakery was charitable in character, and all net receipts of the bakery were used for religious and educational purposes, the entire institution and its activities were properly exempt

[11] *American Medical Association* v. *Board of Review of Department of Labor*, 392 Ill. 614, 65 N.E. 2d 350 (1946).

from the unemployment compensation tax. Justices Givens and Porter joined in a strong dissent, arguing that the exemption should not apply to the commercial activities of the charitable corporation; but on rehearing of the case (in the meantime Chief Justice Holden had resigned and Justice Keeton evidently had reconsidered his opinion), it was found that three members of the court now concurred with the dissent of Justice Givens, thus making it the opinion of the court; and Justice Taylor's opinion, at first concurred in by the majority, now became a lone dissent. The conclusion is that in Idaho the activities of a charitable institution which are clearly within religious, scientific, literary, or educational fields are exempt from unemployment compensation taxation, but activities of a commercial nature carried on by a charitable institution are not exempt, and employees in these commercial activities are entitled to the protection of the unemployment compensation law.[12] The case is of considerable significance because many educational institutions conduct auxiliary enterprises which also serve the general public to some extent; and there is also the possibility that legislative bodies may extend the coverage of unemployment compensation laws to nonprofit institutions.

[12] *In re Gem State Academy Bakery* (Ida.), 224 P. 2d 529 (1950).

CHAPTER XIV

FEDERAL TAXATION

AMONG perennial questions in federal courts are (1) those connected with the computation of the present value of a charitable gift deferred until the death of one or more life annuitants, in order to determine the amount properly deductible from the gross estate as a charitable exemption from the estate tax; and (2) those created by provisions of the instrument of gift authorizing the corpus of a trust, set up for a private beneficiary for a limited time and then to pass to a charitable remainderman, to be invaded for the benefit of the private beneficiary, thereby introducing an element of uncertainty as to the ultimate amount of the charitable gift which would be deductible.

Other questions relate to the administration of the federal income tax in cases where a commercial or industrial plant is sold to a nonprofit college or university and simultaneously leased to the seller, who continues to operate it. These "lease-back" transactions give rise to complex and difficult questions under the Internal Revenue Code. With respect to each litigated transaction: Is it solely a legitimate and ingenious means of investing educational funds for larger returns than would otherwise be possible? Or is it a device to obtain advantages, contrary to the intent of Congress, in the application of the tax statutes to the profit-seeking organization which is a party to it?

THE FEDERAL ESTATE TAX

A donor set up a "living trust," producing an annual income of over $50,000, to provide a $20,000 life annuity for his wife and then to pass to Loyola University in Chicago. In such a case the present value of the charitable gift, for purposes of deduction from the donor's taxable estate at his death, is computed actuarially on the life-expectancy of the annuitant and the probable rate at which interest on the corpus will accrue. The rate of 4 percent being suggested in Treasury Regulation 80, the collector used it and thus arrived at a present value of $806,838 for the deductible charitable legacy. Upon evidence that the bulk of the corpus was actually in municipal and government bonds earning only 2.8 percent and the average annual yield of the entire corpus was only about 3 percent, the United States Court of Claims ordered a recomputation at 3 percent, resulting in a present value of $958,991 and entitling the estate to recover some $36,000 as overpayment of the estate tax. "The Treasury Regulations do not require the use of the 4 per cent factor, and would not be valid if they did, because 4 per cent is obviously at variance with fact." [1]

VALUE OF CHARITABLE REMAINDER AFTER LIFE ESTATE NOT INVARIABLY DETERMINED ACTUARIALLY

A testatrix bequeathed a $300,000 estate in trust to her husband for life, with authority to invade the principal if necessary for his care and maintenance; the remainder after his death was to go to two charities, one of which was Carson-Newman College. Two questions had to be decided by the U.S. Tax Court: (1) Did the permission to invade the principal render the charitable bequests incapable of evaluation at the time of the testatrix' death? (2) If not, must their value be determined in accord with the standard life-expectancy of the husband? The husband, aged 73, was in fact a bedridden hopeless paralytic, expected to die in less than a year, and did die two months after the testatrix. In view of the facts as they existed at the testatrix's death, the court gave negative answers to both questions. The scale on which the couple had lived being well known, the per-

[1] *Hanley* v. *United States* (U.S. Ct. Cl.), 63 F. Supp. 73 (1945), and 63 F. Supp. 95 (1946).

mission to invade the principal could be construed as intended to maintain the husband on the same scale; and the husband's condition being what it was, his life expectancy should be estimated as not exceeding one year. The decision was favorable, therefore, to a relatively high valuation of the deductible charitable bequests.[2]

A 1949 case before the same court, involving Otterbein College in Ohio as one of the charitable remaindermen, and involving also the issue of the life expectancy of an invalid widow aged 85, was similarly decided as to that particular issue. This case also encompassed numerous other complex questions not susceptible of being intelligibly summarized in brief space.[3]

UNLIMITED AUTHORITY TO INVADE CORPUS OF DEFERRED CHARITABLE GIFTS DEFEATS DEDUCTION

A decedent placed his estate in trust for the benefit of his mother during her life, with named charities in Memphis as remaindermen. His mother was 85 at the time of his death, and had $100,000 of her own. These circumstances made it unlikely that she would diminish the corpus of the charitable gift. However, the trust instrument contained words authorizing the corpus to be encroached upon for her benefit, and these words were construed as meaning that the prime purpose of the trust was the mother's "pleasure, comfort and welfare, according to her desires," with no guarantee that anything would go to charity. Accordingly no deduction was allowed.[4]

Since the determination must be made as of the date of the decedent's death, it was immaterial that the mother in fact died at 88, and some $120,000 of her son's estate remained for the charitable legatees. The gist of the decision is well put in the syllabus of the opinion:

[2] *Estate of Nellie H. Jennings*, 10 U.S. Tax Court 323 (1948).

[3] *Huntington National Bank of Columbus, Ohio, and Otterbein College, Transferee of the Estate of Shauck E. Barlow*, 13 U.S. Tax Court 760 (1949).

[4] *Union Planters' National Bank and Trust Company et al. v. Henslee, Collector of Internal Revenue* (U.S.D.C.), 74 F. Supp. 113 (1947).

A deduction for a charitable bequest from a gross estate in computing the estate tax was properly disallowed, where the authority of a life tenant to encroach upon the corpus of the estate was unlimited and no safeguards were set up in the interest of the charitable remainderman, notwithstanding that the age of the life tenant and her independent means made encroachment unlikely.

The decision is in the line of precedents in federal courts which is headed by the case of *Merchants' National Bank of Boston* (1943),[5] as distinguished from the different line headed by the case of *Ithaca Trust Company* v. *United States* (1929),[6] in which a more liberal attitude was adopted. Other cases in both of these groups are digested in *The Colleges and the Courts, 1941–45,* at pages 78–82.

CHARITABLE BEQUEST DEFEATED BY LIMITATION OF TESTAMENTARY POWER IS NOT DEDUCTIBLE

Under Pennsylvania law, charitable bequests made by a Philadelphia testator in a will executed less than thirty days before his death were void. The statute so declaring is an example of a common restriction of the power to make testamentary gifts to charity. In such a case, said the federal district court, no deduction can be claimed for estate tax purposes. The court intimated, however, that if all heirs-at-law of the decedent should file irrevocable disclaimers of any rights in the estate, and indicate their desire that the charitable bequests be executed, then the picture might be different; but this was not the case, and there was no assurance that the intended charitable legatees would ever receive anything under the will.[7]

In another case arising under the same Pennsylvania statute, all heirs and residuary legatees of the testator made and signed an agreement that the charitable bequests, though ineffective under the statute, would nevertheless be paid in full, and the Orphans' Court so ordered, and the bequests were paid. Were

[5] 320 U.S. 256, 64 S. Ct. 108, 88 L. Ed. 35 (1943).
[6] 279 U.S. 151, 49 S. Ct. 291, 73 L. Ed. 647 (1929).
[7] *Selig et al.* v. *United States* (U.S.D.C.), 73 F. Supp. 886 (1947).

they then deductible from the gross estate in computing the federal estate tax? The United States Tax Court denied the deduction. The Pennsylvania statute, said this court, made the bequests *void*. Hence they can not be legacies. The fact that they were paid to the intended legatees was due to an agreement among the actual legatees, and this can not make the original intended bequests valid. Conceding that somewhat similar statutes in Georgia and Ohio have been construed as merely making charitable bequests *voidable* and not wholly *void,* the court adopted a literal view of the Pennsylvania statute, which, indeed, does specify that such bequests shall be void and shall automatically vest in the residuary legatees under the will.[8]

A more recent Tax Court decision, arising under a California statute, takes a more liberal view. The statute makes ineffective a bequest of more than one third of an estate to charity as against a surviving spouse, brother, or sister of the testator. Here a testatrix made such a bequest to three charities, among which was Dartmouth College. Her surviving husband and sister, sole heirs, acquiesced in the will and the estate was distributed in accord with its provisions. The California statute makes such bequests merely *voidable* at the instance of the heirs, and not *void,* said the court, after reviewing the legislative history of the statute and its interpretation in California courts. Therefore in this case, the charitable bequests not having been rendered ineffective, were wholly deductible from the gross estate for federal estate tax purposes. Noting the contrast with the *Estate of Carey* case in which a Pennsylvania statute was involved, the court ascribed it to differences in the wording of the statutes and in their judicial interpretation.[9]

THE FEDERAL INCOME TAX: CLAIMED DEDUCTIBLE LOSS IN SALE AND "LEASE-BACK"

A device sometimes resorted to for the investment of college or university endowment funds in recent years is the purchase

[8] *Estate of William A. Carey,* 9 U.S. Tax Court 1047 (1947).
[9] *Estate of Melusina H. Verick,* 10 U.S. Tax Court 318 (1948)

and "lease-back" of commercial or industrial plants. Sometimes the seller in such a transaction parts with the property at a price far below its book value, intending to claim the difference as a deductible loss in computing his taxable income for the current year. He can also contemplate, at least in some jurisdictions, that the property having passed to a tax-exempt institution will be free from state and local property taxes—a fact which helps to make possible very favorable terms in the lease under which he expects to continue to operate the business while paying annual rentals to the college or university.

In a recent case, an industrial firm conveyed a foundry building and site, valued at $531,710, to William Jewell College in Missouri at a cash price of $150,000, and claimed a deductible loss of $381,710 in computing its income tax. At the same time the firm received a lease of the property for a term of 95 years, subject to cancellation by the lessee after the first 25 years and at the end of each ten-year period thereafter. Under the lease, the lessee would pay insurance premiums on the property, repairs, reconstruction of old buildings and construction of new buildings and improvements. The lessee would also pay all charges against the property for which William Jewell College would be liable as owner if it actually operated the property, "except general state, city, and school taxes," from which the college is exempted by its charter. The lessee would pay to the college rentals aggregating $367,500 for the first 25 years of the lease, varying from $26,400 for the first year to $11,400 for the eleventh year and each year thereafter.

The United States Tax Court held that although the cash price of $150,000 paid by the college was the only consideration mentioned in the deed conveying the property, other evidence made it plain that this was only a part of a more complex single transaction—in other words, that the lease was also an important part of the consideration; that a lease for 95 years is the substantial equivalent of a sale; and therefore that the transaction was essentially an *exchange* of the title for the leasehold. Hence the claimed deductible loss on the cash sale was disallowed. However, the court decided that the claimed loss would be properly allowable as depreciation on the leasehold, spread over the 95-year period of the lease.[10]

THE FEDERAL INCOME TAX: CAPITAL GAINS OF A TRUST ESTATE

Where a testamentary trust was created in 1941, with all income to go to a life beneficiary, and with the remainder at her death to go to Rutgers University, question arose as to whether a capital gain of some $4,000 during a taxable year would be deductible from the gross income for that year, as permanently set aside for an ultimate charitable purpose. The decision was negative, due to the fact that the trustee was directed to invade the corpus whenever the income might fall below $1,500 per month; and there was a strong possibility that this might occur, because during the prosperous war years the annual income was not greatly above that mark. Moreover, since all annual income went to the life beneficiary, there would be no reserve to meet any decrease of income below the mark. Therefore the capital gains could not be treated as permanently dedicated to a charitable purpose, and accordingly were taxable.[11]

IS PRIZE-MONEY WON BY A PROFESSOR TAXABLE AS INCOME?

A professor of music at Brigham Young University composed a symphony during the years 1936–39 and filed it with his other works. It had been his custom to create musical compositions in his spare time, without any design of marketing them or otherwise deriving pecuniary gain from them. In 1946 he reluctantly yielded to the persuasions of his friends and entered his 1939 symphony in a contest to compete for a prize of $25,000 offered by a philanthropist, and the prize was awarded to

[10] *Century Electric Company, Petitioner,* Docket No. 13115, decided in United States Tax Court October 31, 1950.

[11] *Estate of William P. Allen,* 6 U.S. Tax Court 597 (1946).

him in 1947. The Commissioner of Internal Revenue ruled that the prize money was taxable as income, attributable to the years 1945, 1946, and 1947. In 1950 the United States District Court decided that by virtue of Section 22(b) (3) of the Internal Revenue Code the money was not taxable as income for any year.[12] It should be observed that this decision applies only to the particular case and its own set of facts; and it would be hazardous to assume that prize money acquired under varying conditions is never taxable as income.

12 *Robertson* v. *United States* (U.S.D.C.), 93 F. Supp. 660 (1950).

PART FIVE

FINANCIAL SUPPORT FROM PRIVATE SOURCES, INSTITUTIONAL PROPERTY, OTHER MATTERS

CHAPTER XV

THE CREATION OF CHARITABLE TRUSTS

THE first requisite at the inception of a charitable trust is evidence of a charitable intent in the trust instrument. Formerly a degree of certainty of purpose as indicated by at least some specification of a plan of execution was usually held to be essential. But the modern trend is strongly toward sustaining the trust on the basis of general charitable intent alone, with the courts of equity supplying, when necessary, all other details such as appointing a competent trustee and developing, approving, modifying, or otherwise superintending appropriate plans for the operation of the trust. The principle is voiced in a 1948 decision of the New Jersey Court of Chancery: "If the intention be charity, the court will execute the instrument, however vaguely the donor may have indicated his purpose." [1]

UPHOLDING THE TRUST AGAINST ALLEGATIONS OF UNCERTAINTY

Recent decisions in three states exemplify the broad principle. The main issue in a Texas case was the validity of a trust created by the will of a testatrix who did not specify any particular charities or classes of charities but unequivocally stated an intent that her estate of approximately $1,000,000 should become a perpetual charitable trust, with all its income paid to such charities as the trustee bank might designate, after the death of certain persons named as individual recipients of life incomes. The terms of the will were contested as too vague and uncertain to create a valid charitable trust. Indeed they do give

[1] *Y.W.C.A. of Camden* v. *Murrelle* (N.J. Ch.), 56 A. 2d 738 (1948).

the broadest possible discretion to the trustee, but the court sustained the trust, with only Justice Slatton dissenting. His view that "a mere limitation to charity generally, or to charitable uses, is too indefinite" was not shared by any of his colleagues.[2]

In a New Jersey case the donor was only a shade more specific than the testatrix in the Texas case. The Davella Mills Foundation was set up in 1935 as a New Jersey charitable corporation and received immediately a large gift from David B. Mills, who died in 1944, bequeathing his residuary estate to the foundation, "with full power and authority, within the limits imposed by its certificate of incorporation, of selecting the objects of my bounty." The certificate gave authority to expend all the income and all the principal as well,

> consistently with existing laws, for the benefit of an indefinite number of persons, etiher by . . . education or religion, or by relieving their bodies from disease, . . . or by assisting them to establish themselves in life; or by creating or maintaining public buildings or works; or by otherwise lessening the burdens of government.

This closely follows the classic definition of a charitable trust written in 1867 by the famed Justice Gray of Massachusetts. Nevertheless, the will was contested, with the attack centered on a grant of $300,000 made in 1945 by the foundation to incorporate and finance the International Film Foundation, Inc., with the object of "maintenance of world peace by the promotion of better understanding between peoples of different religions, races, and nations." The charitable character of this enterprise was questioned, and an eyebrow was lifted at the $20,000 salary paid to its director. After reviewing all these matters, the New Jersey court of chancery concluded that both of the incorporated enterprises were valid charitable trusts; that the Film Foundation required separate administration; and that there was no evidence that its director was not earning his salary.

[2] *Boyd et al.* v. *Frost National Bank et al.* (Tex.), 196 S.W. 2d 497 (1946).

Moreover, the only issue touching the validity of the will was the charitable character of the bequest to the Mills Foundation; for a valid charitable trust, if maladministered, does not revert to private claimants. Instead, the court will intervene to correct the maladministration and preserve the trust.[3]

Similar principles are illustrated in an Indiana case wherein a decedent who had become wealthy in the course of a business career in Crawfordsville and Montgomery County bequeathed his estate to a bank in trust for general charitable purposes within that city and county, "the objects . . . to be limited only by the good judgment of my trustee; . . . my intention being that the uses shall in general be for public benefit, including relief of worthy poor or distressed persons, for education, religion, and general charitable purposes."

The will also suggested $2,000 a year as a reasonable minimum annual compensation for the trustee and authorized the trustee to bar any prospective beneficiary who made more than one simple request for a grant. As against the attack of the donor's heirs, the will was held to have created a valid charitable trust.[4]

INVALIDITY OF TRUST BECAUSE OF UNCERTAINTY

Not every American jurisdiction has adopted the liberal doctrines enunciated in the foregoing cases regarding certainty in the terms of a trust instrument. For example, in California a will probated in 1944 contained the following words:

> I hereby set aside $5,000 to establish a . . . foundation under the auspices of the Federation of State Societies of California. The purpose of this foundation is to carry on the work of McClellan Reed and his deceased wife, Edna E. Reed, through writings, books, and manuscripts of all kinds and description whatsoever. . . .

This created no trust, said a California Court of Appeal. "Though it is clear that he [testator] intended to create a trust, such attempt was abortive for the reasons (1) no trustee was

[3] *Mills et al.* v. *Montclair Trust Co. et al.* (N.J. Ch.), 49 A. 2d 889 (1946).
[4] *Hulet et al.* v. *Crawfordsville Trust Company* (Ind. App.), 69 N.E. 2d 823 (1946).

designated, and (2) the objects of the trust were not sufficiently explicit and expressed with sufficient certainty to create it." Invoking the words of the California supreme court in a 1934 decision, "where the intention to create a trust is sufficiently expressed, and yet the objects or the subjects of it are uncertain, the gift fails, and the heir or next of kin is let in to the beneficial ownership," the court held that the $5,000 had not been effectively disposed of by the testator, and therefore became a part of his residuary estate.[5]

INVALIDITY WHERE GENERAL CHARITABLE INTENT IS NOT DOMINANT

The will of a decedent who died in 1904 created a trust for the benefit of his granddaughter during her life, with permission to use all the principal, if necessary, for her maintenance; but any remainder was to go to the "Methodist Protestant University of Kansas City (Kansas)." The granddaughter died in 1945. The trust was adjudged to be terminated, and the funds remaining in it ordered distributed to private legatees of the testator, for the following reasons: (1) the testator's dominant intent appeared to have been to assure the support of his granddaughter, (2) the gift of the remainder to the university was *contingent* and *not vested* until the granddaughter's death, and (3) the charitable intent, in so far as it was present, was *specific* and not general, and is defeated by the fact that although the university was once a going concern, it has long since ceased to operate and is now only a nominal entity whose control was transferred in 1926 to the Church of the United Brethren. The fact that the donor's intent was specific, thought the court, precluded any application of the doctrine of *cy pres* in this case, whereby the gift might have been allocated to some similar educational institution or purpose.[6]

[5] *In re Reed's Estate: Parker* v. *Federation of State Societies* (Cal. App.), 186 P. 2d 147 (1947).

[6] *Horton* v. *Board of Education of Methodist Protestant Church et al.* (Wash.), 201 P. 2d 163 (1948).

CONSERVATION OF ASSETS OF A CHARITABLE TRUST DEFERRED TO LET IN A LIFE ESTATE

Interesting comparisons and contrasts with the foregoing case are afforded by a Maryland decision of 1946. Here the decedent gave his widow the income of his residuary estate of about $78,000 for life, with express permission to the trustee bank to invade the corpus "if she needs [it] . . . for living purposes." At her death the trust remainder was to go to Washington College. She had a separate estate of her own worth more than $100,000. During the years 1935–42 she expended for living expenses the income of both estates, plus about $8,500 out of the corpus of her own estate. After 1942 she lived at Santa Fe, New Mexico, on a modest scale, but expended $7,200 a year, which used the income of both estates ($5,900), and left an annual deficit of $1,300. Then, aged 66 and suffering from arthritis, and having no nearer relative than a cousin in New York, she wished to invade the trust corpus to restore the corpus of her own estate and make up the annual deficits. A decree granting this request was reversed by the Maryland Court of Appeals. "While the testator manifested a primary concern for the welfare of his widow," said the court, "he has also shown a solicitude for the conservation of the trust assets," because the permission to invade the corpus was conditioned upon the donee's *need;* hence, the fact of her separate estate was material, and she could not be adjudged in need while she had an estate of $100,000 in her own name, in addition to the trust income.[7]

SUSTAINING A COMPLEX SINGLE TRUST ALLEGED TO BE IN PART NONCHARITABLE

An aged farmer in Illinois bequeathed an estate worth over half a million dollars in a will creating a complicated single trust, primarily concerned with the perpetuation of Funk's

[7] *Board of Visitors and Governors of Washington College* v. *Safe Deposit and Trust Company of Baltimore et al.* (Md.), 46 A. 2d 280 (1946).

Grove Cemetery, a pioneer burial-ground and tourist landmark near the testator's home. The cemetery has long been owned and managed by a stock corporation, technically not charitable, but no dividends have ever been paid or contemplated. The testator's scheme of distribution clearly embodied other purposes purely charitable, as follows: "If and when there becomes a surplus in the trust from income amounting to $150,000 to $200,000, then there shall be a gift to provide for a student union or women's dormitory to be used in connection with Illinois Wesleyan University." and in an intermediate stage between the current care of the cemetery and the accumulation of the foregoing amount of surplus income, "any remaining funds therefrom were to be used to defray the expenses and tuition of young men and women, residents of Dale, Funk's Grove, or Mount Hope Townships in McLean County, as students at the Illinois Wesleyan University at Bloomington or the Illinois State Normal University in Normal."

The heirs-at-law contended that the cemetery trust was void as a private trust in perpetuity, and that the entire scheme of distribution was inseparable and must fall. The Illinois supreme court affirmed a lower court decree dismissing the case, and held the will valid in all respects. The court thought it very doubtful that the cemetery corporation should be regarded as for private pecuniary profit, in view of its history and circumstances; and even if it were, that fact would not necessarily make the trust noncharitable. Further, believed the court, the parts of the scheme were clearly separable, and the unquestionably charitable parts could be upheld separately; but "a charitable intent is apparent throughout the will, and it should be sustained in its entirety," concluded Justice Crampton, for the unanimous court.[8]

[8] *Stubblefield et al.* v. *People's Bank of Bloomington et al.* (Ill.), 94 N.E. 2d 127 (1950).

A GIFT TO A CHARITABLE CORPORATION
IS A CHARITABLE TRUST

A testatrix bequeathed the residue of her estate to an Illinois corporation known as the Bible Institute Colportage Association of Chicago, to be used in the publication and dissemination of evangelical Christian literature in harmony with its articles of incorporation. The bequest was subject to the payment of the necessary expenses of her nephew for life, out of the income only of the residuary estate. The will stipulated that after the death of the nephew "there shall be no further obligation on the part of the Association, and it may then use the entire residue of my estate in the work of the Association, free from all obligations whatsoever."

The Association was merged into the Moody Bible Institute, another Illinois corporation, prior to the death of the testatrix and with her knowledge. Thus by a strained interpretation it was conceivable that the will provided for an outright gift to a corporation not in existence at the testatrix's death, so that the gift would fail and revert to her heirs. But the Indiana appellate court held that the gift was not outright, but in trust for the corporate purposes of the charitable donee; hence the trust would survive the merger of the original donee with another charitable corporation, and the Moody Bible Institute should take the fund under the conditions of the trust.[9]

Judge Royse, though concurring in the result, maintained that the instrument did not create a trust, but made an outright gift. This puzzling position derives from the language used in Bogert on *Trust and Trustees,* and by some other textbook and encyclopedia writers, who seem to state that an unrestricted gift to a charitable donee creates no trust. True enough, it may well create no *special* or *separately defined* trust; but the statement overlooks the elementary fact that charitable corporations hold

[9] *Bible Institute Colportage Association of Chicago et al.* v. *St. Joseph Bank and Trust Company et al.* (Ind. App.), 75 N.E. 2d 666 (1947).

all their assets only for the charitable purposes specified in their charters, and that they can have no assets other than trust assets in that sense. There is probably no real difference among legal scholars on the point; yet where seeming differences appear, as in the dissent in the present case, they are probably on the way toward being resolved by eventual adoption of the broader view held by the majority of the Indiana court.

The supreme court of Tennessee stated this point clearly in a 1905 decision. In case of a gift or bequest to an existing charitable corporation, said the court,

> the trusts need not be set out so specifically and definitely as if made to individuals, in order to make them valid. The reason is that a corporation organized for charitable purposes has these purposes and trusts set out in its charter and articles of foundation, so that the trusts are thus made certain and will control; due deference being paid to the directions of the testator, if any are given. But no trusts in such case need be declared, as they are set out in the charter and articles of foundation.[10]

This is not to infer necessarily that every unrestricted gift must become permanent endowment, or that all assets derived by gifts are beyond the reach of creditors, as the principal of permanent endowment is; it is merely to recognize that all assets of a charitable corporation are impressed with a certain trust character, though this feature includes several variations of kind and degree.

DESIGNATING THE CHARITABLE TRUSTEE

The will of a Kentucky decedent made specific bequests to several living persons, and to several named charities, including Georgetown College in Kentucky. A clause stipulated that "If there should be any balance after the above bequests are paid in full, the remainder is to be divided to those individuals in proportion to the amount named in the bequest as stated above."

[10] *Carson* v. *Carson*, 115 Tenn. 37, 88 S.W. 175 (1905).

The court found no difficulty in deciding that the college would be properly comprehended among "those individuals," and entitled to participate in the residual estate.[11]

NO CHARITABLE TRUST IF TRUSTEE IS GIVEN DISCRETION TO USE THE FUND FOR CHARITABLE OR NON-CHARITABLE PURPOSES IN PERPETUITY

In 1939 a California resident created a "living trust," manifesting an intent to provide for himself and his relatives and to endow a department of philosophy and religion in La Verne College. A family foundation was created to administer the trust, and after the death of the donor in 1947 his heirs contended that the corpus should revert to his estate because the terms of the trust instrument left the trustee corporation free to use the fund for the benefit of certain relatives of the donor at a time extending beyond the limit imposed by the *Statute against Perpetuities;* and that therefore the trust was invalid. After a tortuous course of litigation the California supreme court declared invalid the portion of the trust instrument which purported to benefit the college department of philosophy and religion and which also enabled the trustee at its discretion to devote the income to non-charitable purposes; but the provisions for life annuities to named relatives of the donor, being separable from the foregoing, would stand.[12]

INTENDED TRUST DEFEATED WHEN THE INSTRUMENT CREATING IT IS LEGALLY VOID

No trust is created if the instrument by which it was intended to be set up turns out to be legally void. A woman inherited from her father some six hundred acres of land in Kansas. In 1929 she made a written contract with the Alumni Association of the Kansas State College, agreeing, in honor of her father,

[11] *Georgetown College, Inc.,* v. *Webb et al.,* 313 Ky. 25, 230 S.W. 2d 84 (1950).

[12] *Davenport et al.* v. *Davenport Foundation et al.* (Cal.), 222 P. 2d 11 (1950), affirming in part and reversing in part *Same* (Cal. App.), 215 P. 2d 467 (1950).

to convey the land to the association to provide a fund to aid worthy students. The contract specified that she would make the deeds and deposit them in escrow until her death, whereupon they were to be delivered. There was a further stipulation that the agreement would be revocable by the owner or her husband at any time during her life. In 1938 she made a will devising her entire estate to certain named legatees, and at her death in 1945 it was necessary to determine whether the land was disposed of by the contract and the deeds in escrow, or by the will. An unconditional contract payable at death is enforceable against the maker's estate; but here it was held that the alleged contract, being revocable by its own terms, did not actually bind the maker during her life, and was, in fact, revoked by her will. Moreover, an instrument purporting to convey land only at the death of the maker is held to be testamentary in nature, and therefore invalid unless executed with the formalities required by the law of wills. This holding invalidated the alleged contract and the deeds; and the projected conveyance in trust was a nullity.[13]

In a Maryland case, a decedent had signed a subscription form pledging one third of her estate to American University in Washington, D.C., to become due on the day of her death and to be paid within one year thereafter. She died intestate, and hence the question of the enforceability of the subscription pledge was clear-cut. The trial court dismissed American University's claim, and this judgment was affirmed by the Court of Appeals, holding that the subscription could not be given effect because it was an attempted testamentary disposition of property, but not executed in accord with the statutory formalities appertaining to wills, and was therefore void.[14] Judge Delaplaine dissented, believing the subscription should be treated as a contract, and not as an attempted will. He pointed out that the instrument contained a promise by the university to create a

[13] *In re Smith's Estate; Dressler et al.* v. *Alumni Association of the Kansas State College et al.* (Kan.), 175 P. 2d 1012 (1946).

[14] *American University* v. *Collings et al.* (Md.), 59 A. 2d 333 (1948).

memorial fund to bear the name of the subscriber in this case, and thought that this reciprocal promise was sufficient to make the pledge a binding contract rather than merely an intended gift.

CHAPTER XVI

THE EXECUTION OF EDUCATIONAL TRUSTS

CASES digested in this chapter are concerned with the operation of charitable trusts for higher education, as distinguished from questions as to their validity, which receive attention in the preceding chapter. The execution of educational trusts also receives further treatment in the next following chapter, dealing with recent applications of the judicial doctrine of *cy pres*.

WHEN THE TRUSTEE IS EMPOWERED TO SELECT THE LOCATION

In 1941 a wealthy Chicagoan died, naming a Chicago bank as trustee of his residual estate of approximately $1,250,000, to establish in his native state of Missouri an educational institution to bear his name and to offer technological training "with a view of better equipping young men and women for performing the world's work." The trustee was expressly empowered to determine the location within the state of Missouri, and the will recited that "Boston Tech of Boston or Rice Institute of Houston would exemplify" the testator's intent.

The trustee bank sought and obtained in 1943 a decree of the Chicago superior court directing it to hold and invest the fund pending further steps and reserving jurisdiction to hear further evidence on the selection of the location. The bank then appointed a committee of three men to receive applications and make recommendations. In March 1944 this committee reported: two of its members recommended that the school be located at St. Louis University and one recommended that it be at Washington University in St. Louis. In April the bank reported to the court that it had selected Washington University.

In June the superior court issued a second decree directing the bank to hold the fund in perpetuity for the Sever Institute of Geophysical Technology, to be established as an autonomous school of St. Louis University, thus nullifying the bank's determination. This decree was reversed, however, by the Illinois appelate court, which noted that the will plainly gave the trustee power to choose the location. In such cases a court of equity has jurisdiction to advise or assist the trustee but not to substitute its own judgment for that of the trustee, except where there is proof of malice, fraud, or bad faith. Thus the bank's choice of university must stand.[1]

ADHERING TO THE DONOR'S DOMINANT PURPOSE

A will probated in 1922 set up a trust for the benefit of several private beneficiaries until the death of the last survivor among them, and named the Asheville Normal and Associated Schools as remainderman. If this institution should not be in existence at the time, then the trust was to pass to Ohio Wesleyan University as endowment for its department of chemistry. It turned out that the charitable bequest did not become operative until 1945. By that time three of the four units of the Asheville institution had long since closed their doors. One unit, the Asheville Farm School, continued and was operated together with a girls' school and a college, all under the name of Warren Wilson College. The only incorporated agency in the whole history was the body now known as the Board of National Missions of the Presbyterian Church in the United States of America, by which the schools were sponsored and controlled. It was adjudged that Ohio Wesleyan University could claim no interest in the legacy because (1) a bequest to an unincorporated legatee will be sustained as a gift to the incorporated parent organization, where there is one; and (2) the Asheville institu-

[1] *Continental Illinois National Bank and Trust Company of Chicago* v. *Sever (St. Louis University et al., Interveners)* (Ill.), 65 N.E. 2d 385 (1946), affirming *Same; Murtaugh* v. *Washington University,* 324 Ill. App. 613, 59 N.E. 2d 197 (1945).

tions have had a continuous existence under different names and have served and are serving substantially the testator's primary purpose, which was to aid the program of Christian education for the youth of the mountain area in western North Carolina as he had observed it.[2]

A recent surrogate decision in New York exemplifies somewhat similar principles. A decedent in Oneida bequeathed $500 to the Hebrew Free School in Utica, an unincorporated association. Subsequent to the execution of the will, the school changed its name and location, and eventually was absorbed by and became a part of a charitable corporation known as the Jewish Community Council of Utica, N.Y., Inc. In these circumstances it was held that although in New York an unincorporated association can not take or hold property, this fact does not invalidate a charitable bequest. The courts of equity have power to appoint a trustee to carry out the charitable intent. Accordingly it was ordered that the Jewish Community Council is entitled to take the bequest in this case.[3]

EXPENSES OF LITIGATION WHERE DISPUTANTS ARE CHARITABLE INSTITUTIONS

"A trust fund of right should bear the expenses of its own administration" is something of a maxim. It is often difficult to determine precisely what expenses are legitimately chargeable, however. Where the trust instrument is ambiguous, so that two or more litigants may fairly make adverse claims to the fund, all the disputants being charitable institutions, a Missouri court holds that the costs of the litigation and reasonable attorneys' fees for both the defeated and successful parties may be allowed out of the trust estate. This would not apply to litigants attacking the validity of the trust or suing to get private possession of its assets.[4]

[2] *Wachovia Bank and Trust Company* v. *Board of National Missions of Presbyterian Church in U.S.A.*, 226 N.C. 546, 39 S.E. 2d 621 (1946).

[3] *In re Levine* (N.Y. Sur.), 98 N.Y.S. 2d 680 (1950).

[4] *Lang et al.* v. *Taussig et al.* (Mo.), 192 S.W. 2d 407 (1946), transferred to (Mo. App.), 194 S.W. 2d 743 (1946).

INVESTMENT OF ENDOWMENT FUNDS

During the last twenty years, a great and apparently permanent decline in the general level of interest rates and the ups and downs of the cycle of deflation and inflation have complicated the problems of trustees endeavoring to safeguard the value of trust property and obtain regular and dependable income therefrom. A recent case involved a trust in New Hampshire set up to provide incomes for named private beneficiaries for a period of forty years and thereafter to go to designated charitable remaindermen. The donor's words in the trust instrument were: "I direct it shall be invested in at least two good savings banks in New Hampshire."

The trustee bank asked for a decree to broaden its discretion as to investment, upon showing that the average savings bank interest rate had declined from 4.15 percent in 1932, the year of the testator's death, to 1.99 percent in 1945, thus cutting in half the income which he probably anticipated; and the supreme court of New Hampshire agreed that "This could be found to be a change in circumstances unforeseen by the testator that substantially impairs the accomplishment of the gift of the income."

Considering whether investment in common stocks should be here authorized, the court quoted from Scott on Trusts:

> The question has arisen whether the trustee should be permitted to invest in common stocks, although by the terms of the trust or by statute these are not proper trust investments, on the ground that in the event of monetary inflation such stocks would presumably rise in value and would therefore be a hedge against inflation.
>
> In states in which the purchase of properly selected shares of stock is a legal trust investment and the terms of the trust do not forbid such purchase, there is no difficulty. In such a case the trustee is merely required to exercise a proper degree of prudence under the circumstances. Undoubtedly the danger of inflation is a circumstance which a trustee can and should take into account in determining whether and to what extent he should invest in the purchase of shares of stock.

Resuming its own discourse, the court concluded:

> Substantially lower interest rates should be carefully considered by a trustee and the court of equity as well as the factor of inflation. The one as well as the other results in loss that is an impairment of the gifts of a trust. It is true that [in this case] the lower dividends of the savings banks affect only the life tenants, but their rights must be protected as well as those of the remaindermen. This state permits trustees to invest in common stocks within limits and the will here does not forbid it although it directs depositing in savings banks.[5]

A section of the Personal Property Law of New York authorizes the courts to give appropriate instructions when trustees present facts tending to show that specific personal property must be sold for the good of the trust, but a court is under no compulsion to give long-term blanket or general authority to sell, and at least one court has refused to do so.

An unnamed charitable trust, created in 1911 under an instrument directing that $31,000 in West Shore Railroad 4 percent bonds be held until matured (in the year 2015) or paid, asked the court "to permit it, at its discretion and without further direction from the court, at any time and from time to time, to sell and dispose of" the bonds. Finding that the bonds had always paid interest regularly and were currently selling at 84¼, the court curtly noted that "The construction sought would completely change the scheme apparent from the face of the trust deed," and "Giving the trustee the powers asked for would not amount to a construction but a destruction of the obvious intent of the settlor of the trust." [6]

EXECUTING EXPLICIT MANDATORY TERMS OF THE TRUST INSTRUMENT

An estate including much valuable real property was given by will in trust to Lehigh University, with the explicit stipulation

[5] *Citizens' National Bank* v. *Morgan et al.* (N.H.), 51 A. 2d 841 (1947).

[6] *Application of United States Trust Company of New York, in re Griffith et al.* (Misc.), 66 N.Y.S. 2d 72 (1946).

that none of the property should be sold except by permission of the orphans' court of Northampton County and after the university trustees filed a bond that the proceeds would be invested in improvements on the remaining properties. The testator gave one of his old employees a life estate in one dwelling house, after which the house would become a part of the university trust. The university sold its interest in this house to the life tenant without seeking permission of the court. Questioning the security of his title, he withheld a part of the purchase price, and when the university sued to recover that sum, his defense that the university could not convey clear title because it had not compiled with the terms of the will was held to be good. The will, said the court, did not convey the property to the university in fee simple for its general corporate purposes, but created an active special trust which must be operated subject to the specified conditions.[7]

Two North Carolina decisions of 1947 and 1948 were concerned with the will of Maxwell Chambers, a benefactor of Davidson College who died in 1855. One clause of the will gave, in trust, to the Elders of the First Presbyterian Church in Salisbury certain lots adjacent to the church property "reserving and withholding from them the right of selling the same or any part of them," and expressing a desire that the church should partition off the lots and improve them with suitable buildings which could be leased to produce income. It was stipulated that in the event of failure of this trust, the property should pass to Davidson College.

In 1947 the elders of the church came into court alleging they were unable to manage the valuable lots properly, and asking for a declaratory judgment authorizing them to sell the lots. The Chambers heirs filed a cross-action demanding that Davidson College now be required to assert its rights or disavow any claim to the property. Thereupon the college filed a plea for the protection of its rights in the matter. When the tripartite

[7] *Lehigh University* v. *Hower* (Pa. Super.), 46 A. 2d 516 (1946).

action reached the supreme court of North Carolina, it was dismissed as improperly brought under the Declaratory Judgments Act. What the parties needed, said Chief Justice Stacey, was the advice and direction of a court of equity in the administration of the testamentary trust.[8]

Subsequently the interested parties all agreed that the best solution would be to effect an exchange of the church's fee-simple property in Church Square (adjacent to the lots in question) for property of equal value in Parsonage Square (which latter property the elders also held in trust under the will of Maxwell Chambers), so as to bring the whole of Church Square under the terms of the Chambers trust. To this was added the condition that the church should be allowed to use the church building in Church Square rent-free until a new church building could be erected in Parsonage Square. In a suit against the attorney general to obtain approval of this plan, a favorable judgment was rendered by the trial court, and affirmed by the state supreme court.[9]

[8] *Brandis et al.* v. *Trustees of Davidson College et al.*, 227 N.C. 329, 41 S.E. 2d 833 (1947).

[9] *Brandis et al.* v. *McMullan, Attorney General*, 229 N.C. 411, 50 S.E. 2d 7 (1948).

CHAPTER XVII

SOME APPLICATIONS OF THE JUDICIAL DOCTRINE OF CY PRES

WHERE a trust instrument evinces clearly a general charitable intent, but contains directions which, if literally adhered to, would defeat or seriously cripple the execution of that desire, courts of equity may modify the directions so as to make possible the operation of the trust for the accomplishment of the charitable purpose as nearly as practicable in accord with the donor's wishes. This is the doctrine of *cy pres*. Its theoretical basis varies somewhat in different jurisdictions, and its applications depend upon the circumstances in each case. A few recent examples follow.

THE GENERAL CHARITABLE PURPOSE MAY SURMOUNT IMPRACTICABLE SPECIFICATIONS

A recent case in New Jersey chancery illustrates this matter well. A testator possessed eight volumes of loose-leaf typed notes entitled "Random Scientific Notes Seeking the Essentials in Place and Space," written by himself. He directed his executors to expend $15,000 to edit, type or print, and distribute 100 copies of this document, and he provided for a trust fund of $150,000 to be offered successively and alternatively to the National Academy of Sciences at Washington, Princeton University, Harvard University, California Institute of Technology, and the American Philosophical Society at Philadelphia, on condition that the recipient raise within three years another $150,000, the income from both funds to be used "to continue and carry forward to completion and to publish for popular understanding" his researches as recorded in the "Random Notes." In case none of these first five offerees accepted the trust, then the $150,000 bequest was to be offered to the League of Nations at Geneva or, alternatively, to Princeton University, on any terms satisfactory to his executors.

Examination of the "Notes" by distinguished professors of philosophy and of science produced unanimous reports to the effect that the document was unsystematic and unscientific, largely incoherent and unintelligible, in part irrational, and meaningless and worthless as a contribution to knowledge or as a basis for further investigations. It appeared that the testator had been touched with megalomania and had entertained inflated notions regarding the importance of his thoughts and writings.

The National Academy of Sciences renounced any rights under the will. The League of Nations and its successor, the United Nations, rejected the gift. Princeton University declined to accept the trust under the first stated terms but argued that the fund should be given to its department of philosophy as an endowment for philosophical investigations and research. Heirs of the testator contend that the trust was not charitable, because the testator's ruling intent was merely to ensure the publication of his own writings and to perpetuate his own name and that, therefore, the trust should fail and the fund revert to the estate.

Faced with these facts and these contentions, the court examined the whole will and found numerous expressions indicating a wish to do something "for the benefit of all mankind" and for "world benefit," clearly classifiable as a general charitable intent. The testator had been mistaken in his choice of a specific means of effectuating that intent, but the case seemed to be a peculiarly apt one for the application of *cy pres*.

Accordingly, the court directed the executors that neither the $15,000 nor any other sum should be expended for reproducing the "Notes" and held that the intended gift of the $150,000 fund created a valid charitable trust that was impossible of execution according to its particular terms but should be preserved and executed by naming Princeton University as trustee, with the income of the fund to be used for philosophical researches by the Princeton department of philosophy.[1]

RETARDING OR ACCELERATING THE TIMING OF DIRECTED ACTS

In Kentucky a decedent in 1945 created a trust estate having a value of $3,885,000, producing an annual income of $125,-000 to $150,000. The estate included 14,000 acres of land, and the will directed the development of an arboretum thereon, and the construction of a museum building of a specified type at a cost of $300,000 as soon as the corpus should reach a value exceeding $3,500,000. Development of a 450-acre arboretum pursuant to the will, at a substantial annual outlay, was begun and carried on; but it was found that the erection of a museum building of the kind planned would cost at least $800,000. The donor's instructions regarding the museum appeared to have become impracticable of immediate execution on account of unforeseen changes in economic conditions. Accordingly a decree authorizing the trustee to defer the building of the museum was affirmed by the Kentucky Court of Appeals.[2]

In Alabama an instrument creating a trust for educational purposes contemplated the establishment of a school of a specified type for white boys, and contained a "backlog provision" directing that this project should be initiated after the trust fund began to produce a specified amount of annual income. In the judgment of some of the governors of the trust this provision, if literally followed, would unduly delay the effectuation of the charitable intent; and a decree was sought to authorize

1 *Wilber* v. *Asbury Park National Bank and Trust Company et al.* (N.J. Ch.), 59 A. 2d 570 (1948).

2 *Citizens' Fidelity Bank and Trust Company* v. *Isaac W. Bernheim Foundation,* 305 Ky. 802, 205 S.W. 2d 1003 (1947).

them to proceed with the establishment of a unit of the projected school. Affirming a favorable decree of the lower court, the supreme court of Alabama held that, considering the will as a whole and the surrounding circumstances, the "backlog provision" should be construed as not mandatory, but merely administrative and directory, and subject to the doctrine of equitable deviation.[8]

The trust instrument contained a proviso that if after the lapse of 25 years the school project shall be determined unsuccessful, then all the trust property is to be liquidated, and one half of it given to the Massachusetts Institute of Technology for educational purposes under specified conditions, and the other half held in trust for educational aid to boys under the age of 21; and if the Massachusetts Institute of Technology should not accept the gift with the specified conditions, then all should go to the latter purpose. The donor died in 1930, and the decree of 1947 directed the governors of the trust to proceed to erect and operate the first unit of the school project. The trust is known as the Alabama Educational Foundation.

ADHERING AS CLOSELY AS POSSIBLE TO THE DONOR'S ORIGINAL INTENT

The case of the Ackland Memorial Art Museum, discussed at page 107 in *The Colleges and the Courts, 1941–45,* under the caption of *Noel et al.* v. *Olds et al.,* was left in the hands of the federal District Court in 1945, the principal remaining issue being that of whether the University of North Carolina or Rollins College should be designated as the site of the projected museum, after Duke University had declined to accept the trust. Accordingly the court ordered the trustees of the estate to make a recommendation on that question. After two years the trustees reported in favor of the University of North Carolina, citing as reasons (1) This university had by far the greater financial stability—a factor known to have been in the mind of the donor,

[8] *Thurlow et al.* v. *Berry et al.,* 247 Ala. 361, 32 So. 2d 526 (1947).

and (2) Both the university and its location were most nearly similar to the type of institution and locale favored by the donor when he designated Duke University in his will.

Notwithstanding this recommendation, the District Court nevertheless designated Rollins College, on the ground that it was "more of an art center" than the University of North Carolina, and because there was evidence, nontestamentary in character, that the donor was sentimentally attached to the college, and at one time orally mentioned it as his second choice. Upon appeal, this judgment was ordered set aside. The United States Court of Appeals, after weighing the evidence in the lengthy record, concluded that the donor's intent placed great emphasis upon financial stability and upon a location geographically suited for advancement of the cause of art in the South, and decided that the University of North Carolina should be designated, and remanded the case with direction to enter a decree to that effect.[4]

COGNIZANCE OF CHANGED CIRCUMSTANCES

"Equity may mold the trust" compresses in an apothegm the principle that courts of equity may authorize modifications in the terms of a trust instrument if and when by reason of changed conditions the terms become impossible or impracticable of performance but may be modified to approximate the donor's charitable intent. In 1918 Louis Comfort Tiffany set up a "living trust" of over $1,000,000 to establish and maintain an art school and museum in Oyster Bay, New York, consisting of some 62 acres of wooded grounds and appropriate buildings. It was operated in flourishing condition for several years, but in the early 1930s its income and the numbers of students in attendance greatly declined. By 1942 there were only eight students, and the buildings were turned over for temporary war use to the National Defense Research Council. When that agency relinquished them after the war, the future of the institution had

[4] *Olds et al.* v. *Rollins College; University of North Carolina* v. *Rollins College* (U.S.C.A. for D.C.), 173 F. 2d 639 (1949).

to be considered and determined. The court gave permission to sell the real and personal property, add the proceeds to the capital of the trust, and use the income for fellowships for creative work in the fine arts. Thus, the art school may physically disappear, but its generic purpose will be carried on. Certain questions concerning investment of the funds were reserved for later decision by the court when the occasion arises.[5]

Where is the line between "molding the trust" and absolute failure of the trust because it is impossible to approximate the donor's intent? A testatrix who died in 1926 devised property worth about $50,000 in trust to three women trustees, to be offered to the University of Wisconsin to endow a chair of American history to be held by a woman with the rank and emoluments of full professor and salary of not less than $6,000 a year. The regents of the university accepted the proposal and nominally created the chair by resolutions of 1930 and 1931, but in 1937 voted to reconsider and reject the gift. By 1944 the property had deteriorated to about half its original value, and the annual expenses of administration under the three women trustees always exceeded the income. Heirs of the testatrix sued to recover the property on the ground that the trust was impossible of execution. The Wisconsin supreme court thought the regents could not reject what they had formerly accepted, but that their acceptance bound them only to establish and maintain the professorship, without undertaking the burden of administering its endowment fund unless they so desired. Noting that the current cost of administering trust property under the regents was about one seventh of one percent, the court ordered that the regents be offered appointment as successor trustees to the three women, with all their powers and duties. In case the regents accept, the trust will survive; if they decline, then a judgment declaring the trust a failure and awarding the property to the testatrix's heirs was directed.[6]

[5] *Application of Arms et al., in re Louis Comfort Tiffany Foundation* (N.Y. Sup.), 64 N.Y.S. 2d 693 (1946).

[6] *In re Robinson's Estate* (Wis.), 21 N.W. 2d 391 (1946).

Something of an anticlimax was the 1947 decision of a New York court that Teachers College, Columbia University, was authorized to close its combined Lincoln School–Horace Mann School in 1948, and devote the real property and endowment of the Lincoln School, not to the operation of an experimental school, but to an institute of school experimentation to carry on projects in cooperation with associate schools or school systems in various communities throughout the country. Anticlimax, because essentially the same issues had been determined in an earlier decision permitting the merging of the Lincoln School with the Horace Mann School, despite a clause in the deed of gift from the General Education Board which committed the $3,000,000 endowment to "the support of the Lincoln School of Teachers College in order to insure permanence of experimental work in the field of elementary and secondary education."

Not only did the General Education Board appear as a party and consent to the judgment; it was also shown that at the time of the gift the board had in force written policies to the effect that donees should, after the lapse of ten years, have discretion to modify or change the purposes of the gift provided only they adhered as closely as practicable to the original purposes. After hearing extensive expert educational testimony, the court decided that experience and changing conditions indicated that the new purpose would be more likely to conduce toward optimum accomplishment of the original intent than would the continued operation of the Lincoln School, and entered judgment accordingly.

The judgment was modified (but without changing its essential effect) by the Appellate Division, when Justice Van Voorhis and his four colleagues agreed that the decision as to the use of the endowment fund, though correct, was not an application of the doctrine of *cy pres,* because in view of differences of opinion among educators the court could scarcely conclude that the continued use of the endowment income for the former purpose was impossible or impracticable; but as to the real property of the school, the decision was a true application of *cy pres* because after the trustees determined to exercise their option of using the endowment income for a different purpose, then the continued operation of the school plant for its former purpose was obviously impracticable. As modified, the judgment was subsequently affirmed by the New York Court of Appeals.[7]

[7] *Teachers College* v. *Goldstein et al.*, 297 N.Y. 969, 80 N.E. 2d 357 (1948), affirming *Same*, 273 App. Div. 11, 75 N.Y.S. 2d 250 (1947), which modified and affirmed *Same* (Misc.), 70 N.Y.S. 2d 778 (1947).

CHAPTER XVIII

THE TORT RESPONSIBILITY OF COLLEGES AND UNIVERSITIES

DAMAGE suits against universities and colleges appeared only rarely in the higher courts during 1946–50. Probably the most significant decision was that of the supreme court of Illinois, holding that the doctrine of charitable immunity, though still the law in Illinois and still upheld by the weight of American judicial opinion, may be properly construed as not preventing recovery from an institution which is protected by liability insurance so that its charitable trust funds will not be touched.

RECOVERY AGAINST CHARITABLE INSTITUTION COVERED BY LIABILITY INSURANCE

In May 1940 a girl student at Bradley Polytechnic Institute (now Bradley University) at Peoria sustained injuries when a trapeze assembly on which she was practicing an act for the college circus fell with her to the hardwood floor of the gymnasium. She sued the instructor in charge and the Institute for negligence. The trial court concluded that the action against the Institute must be dismissed because of its immunity as a charitable institution; whereupon an attempt was made to appeal directly to the state supreme court on the ground that the rule of charitable immunity violates the state and federal constitutions. The supreme court declined to review the case and transferred the appeal to the intermediate appellate court, which handed down a decision in 1948 sustaining the rule of charitable immunity as enunciated in the classic Illinois case of *Parks* v. *Northwest-*

ern University (1905),[1] and holding that the fact that the Institute carried liability insurance was of no consequence in determining its liability. Appeal was then taken to the supreme court, resulting in reversal.

Chief Justice Thompson, speaking for the majority of the court, declared that the doctrine of charitable immunity, as in the *Parks Case,* had for its sole object the protection of charitable trust funds; and that a tort action may be brought against a charitable corporation where it appears that its trust funds will not be impaired or depleted by the prosecution of the complaint. This, said he, is not an abandonment of the rule in the *Parks Case,* but a proper extension of it. "Reason and justice require an attempt to inject some humanitarian principles into the abstract rule of absolute immunity," said he. "The law is not static and must follow and conform to changing conditions and new trends in human relations to justify its existence as a servant and protector of the people; and, when necessary, new remedies must be applied where none exist." [2]

The court explicitly refrained from indorsing the abolition of charitable immunity, as persuasively advocated from a federal court of appeals bench by the late Justice Wiley Rutledge in his famed opinion in the *Georgetown University Case* of 1942.[3]

Not impressed by the reasoning of the majority of the court, Justices Crampton and Wilson dissented, arguing that "The primary issue of immunity should be frankly faced and the reasons and justification which support it should be re-examined in the light of fundamental common-law principles."

The case marks another stage in the chipping away of the harsh rule of immunity which has hitherto generally denied

[1] Digested in *The Colleges and the Courts* (1936), at pp. 421–22. Cited as 218 Ill. 381, 75 N.E. 991, 2 L.R.A.N.S. 556, 4 Ann. Cas. 103 (1905).

[2] *Moore* v. *Moyle et al.,* 405 Ill. 555, 92 N.E. 2d 81 (1950), *reversing Same,* 335 Ill. App. 342, 82 N.E. 2d 61 (1948).

[3] Digested in *The Colleges and the Courts, 1941–45,* at pp. 119–120. Cited as *President and Directors of Georgetown College* v. *Hughes* (U.S.C.A. for D.C.), 130 F. 2d 810 (1942).

indemnity to innocent aggrieved parties when the injury was due to the negligence of a charitable institution or its agents.

ALLEGED NEGLIGENCE MUST BE THE PROXIMATE CAUSE OF THE INJURY

Sometimes in a tort action against a college or university the court is able to avoid altogether the question of immunity, because the complainant's case fails for other reasons which would be fatal even if the defendant were not a charitable institution. Such a case was a recent one involving Baylor University. Baylor's main campus is at Waco, but it operates a medical school and hospital at Dallas. The hospital had in practice a reciprocal arrangement with another hospital at San Angelo, whereby blood donations were collected at San Angelo and shipped to Dallas, where the Baylor Hospital processed the blood into blood plasma, and furnished the San Angelo hospital with blood plasma. Baylor also furnished the San Angelo hospital a "collecting unit," consisting of bottles, towels, tubing, a needle to go into a vein of the donor's arm, and a smaller needle to inject a hypodermic to make the arm insensitive to pain. These articles were sterilized and packed at Dallas, and not resterilized at San Angelo.

The plaintiff was a blood-donor at San Angelo who suffered a chronic infection in her arm following her phlebotomy (blood donation) in 1946, and alleged that her injury was caused by the negligence of the hospital in performing the phlebotomy with an unsterile needle, which had been negligently furnished for the purpose by Baylor University. Although it was clear that the plaintiff did indeed suffer an infection, and that the hospital at San Angelo gave her twelve days' free hospitalization and treatment without effecting a cure, the evidence was not deemed conclusive as to whether or not the infection had actually been caused by an infected needle. Accordingly the judgment of the trial court in favor of the defendants, based on a directed verdict, was affirmed, on the ground that the plaintiff had failed to prove that the alleged negligence was the proximate cause of the injury.[4]

INJURIES ALLEGED TO BE DUE TO ATOMIC FISSION

A case originating at the University of Rochester in 1946 is of little legal significance, because it was compromised out of court after some preliminary sparring. A bookkeeper, employed in a federally supervised project other than the Manhattan District and having no connection with it, alleged that he worked in the university building where the cyclotron was housed and in such close proximity to it that he was injured by radioactive protons thrown off by it. His petition for a writ of discovery to obtain certain sources of evidence from the university was granted in part, but his prayer to compel the university to produce samples of uranium 235 and plutonium for inspection was denied, because the university as contractor with the War Department was merely custodian and not owner of these substances in minute quantities, and the War Department's security regulations precluded the exhibiting of samples. In another series of orders connected with this case, a motion by the defendant for a physical examination of the plaintiff, including x-ray photos, urinalysis, blood sample, sample of food contents of stomach, and bone marrow biopsy, was granted.[5]

[4] *Brown et ux.* v. *Shannon West Texas Memorial Hospital and Baylor University* (Tex. Civ. App.), 222 S.W. 2d 248 (1949).

[5] *Cardinal* v. *University of Rochester et al.* (Misc.), 63 N.Y.S. 2d 868 (1946), modified and affirmed (App. Div.), 69 N.Y.S. 2d 355 (1947); and *Same,* 188 Misc. 823, 71 N.Y.S. 2d 614 (1946), 271 App. Div. 1048, 69 N.Y.S. 2d 352 (1947), and (Misc.), 71 N.Y.S. 2d 617 (1947).

CHAPTER XIX

INSTITUTIONAL REAL PROPERTY

THE recent cases are concerned with a variety of matters, including (1) the right of educational institutions to alienate or encumber real estate under varying circumstances, (2) use of the power of eminent domain by and against universities, (3) the impact of municipal zoning regulations upon private colleges, and (4) sundry questions relating to property rights on state university campuses.

STATE SCHOOL AND INSTITUTIONAL LANDS

The state of Arizona has some 9,000,000 acres of public lands dedicated to schools and other institutions, and an endowment fund of some $5,000,000 derived from sales of a small portion of these lands. As to such of these lands as were granted by the federal government, the methods by which they may be sold are prescribed in the Enabling Act (the act of Congress under which Arizona was admitted to the Union in 1912); and the state constitution extends these same provisions to "all lands otherwise acquired by the state."

Litigation arose in an instance where the state, owning a tract of land acquired by foreclosure on a loan from the permanent school fund, *exchanged* this tract for another held by a private owner. When later the title to the tract which the state had thus alienated came into question, a judgment ordering the deed of exchange canceled was affirmed by the supreme court, because this method of disposing of public lands held in trust for educational purposes is not authorized. "Lands acquired on foreclosure are identified as proceeds of the original trust *res*, and belong to the trust estate and are subject to the conditions of the trust." Accordingly the deed was a nullity, as was also a mortgage given by the holder of the deed; and the mortgagee, an insurance company, could not recover. "Estoppel does not apply to the state, regarding *ultra vires* acts of state officials." [1]

Discoursing further on the management of investments derived from the public lands, the court went on to note that the Enabling Act gives the state treasurer (with the approval of the governor and the secretary of state) full discretion to purchase "safe, interest-bearing securities," and does not make him liable as an insurer of the trust funds. The legislature, said the court, has no power to advise or direct the treasurer regarding these investments; but the history of the matter shows heavy investments and considerable losses in mortgages, bought because of legislative and popular pressure. One instance cited was that of the breaking of the Lyman Dam on the Little Colorado River in 1915, when many tracts on which the state held mortgages were ruined.

ENCUMBRANCE AND ALIENATION OF REAL PROPERTY BY PRIVATELY CONTROLLED INSTITUTIONS

Shaw University in Raleigh, North Carolina, decided to mortgage certain of its buildings and sites to secure a loan of $200,000 for the purpose of erecting new buildings and repairing others, all to be used for its educational purposes. In a test case, the supreme court affirmed a finding that the university could execute a valid mortgage. The land in question had been acquired originally in 1870 by deed of gift in fee simple, with authority to "use, rent, or sell," but always to apply the proceeds to its educational uses. There was no reverter clause in the deed. The charter of Shaw University empowers it to construct, remodel, furnish and equip buildings, and "to borrow money . . . and execute mortgages, deeds of trust, and other

[1] *Murphy et al.* v. *State* (Ariz.), 181 P. 2d 336 (1947).

pledge agreements, on both personal and real property, as security for money so borrowed." [2]

Porter Academy in Charleston, South Carolina, received its campus by deed of the Secretary of War in 1888, with a clause providing for reverter if not used for educational purposes. A new deed, authorized by a special act of Congress, was given by the Secretary of the Army in 1949, making the grant unconditional and renouncing the reverter clause. Needing money to pay debts, operating expenses, and finance plant improvements, the Academy wished either to mortgage its entire plant for about $150,000, or to sell two apartment houses on the campus and mortgage the remainder of the plant for $75,000. Said the supreme court of South Carolina, "The Porter Academy has power to sell any or all of the property, upon its determination that such sale would serve the purposes of the said Porter Academy, and it is within its power to prevent default and foreclosure by such sales as are deemed by it to be necessary." [3]

WHEN IS A LEASE EQUIVALENT TO A SALE?

Sayre College acquired its campus in Lexington, Kentucky, in 1860 by a deed of gift in fee simple, "without power of alienation or encumbrance." Recently it was deemed necessary to lease certain unused parts of the land to produce income to keep the college in operation. Accordingly an action was brought for a declaration of rights, to authorize the college to enter into two leases: one for ten years with option of renewal for another ten years, and one for 99 years.

The Kentucky Court of Appeals readily held that the ten-year lease is not an "encumbrance" within the meaning of the deed, and that the college has power to make such a lease; but the 99-year lease would be an "alienation" within the meaning of the deed, and is prohibited. This latter conclusion was the

[2] *Shaw University* v. *Durham Life Insurance Company*, 230 N.C. 526, 53 S.E. 2d 656 (1949).

[3] *Frierson* v. *Porter Academy et al.* (S.C.), 60 S.E. 2d (1950).

more easily reached because the proposed 99-year lease called for a monetary consideration of only $10,000, all of which was to be paid within three years, leaving a period of 96 years during which the property would be controlled by the lessee and produce no income for the college. Said the court, "A lease of this sort approaches a sale of the property," and expressed unwillingness to "leave the property handicapped with this long-term non-productive lease." Conceding its own power to authorize such a transaction under the doctrine of *cy pres,* the court thought the evidence of essentiality was insufficient, and commented that $10,000 would hardly save the college if it were really in serious financial straits. Another element was the fact that the original deed named the General Assembly of the Presbyterian Church in the United States as successor trustee in the event that the corporation of Sayre College should fail to execute the purposes of the trust.[4]

EMINENT DOMAIN

Recent litigation includes one case in which a state university acquired a parcel of property by condemnation, and another in which a privately controlled university lost property to a municipal corporation exercising the right of eminent domain. The opinions in both cases are largely concerned with ancillary procedural matters not of great general significance.

A private owner of certain land which the University of Alabama was authorized to acquire by condemnation, by order of the probate court, sought to obtain from the higher courts a supervisory writ to halt the transaction. When his petition reached the supreme court through proper channels of appeal, it was held that the relator had defeated his own rights by *laches,* having delayed seven months, apparently in the hope of getting a new probate judge to act on a matter which had al-

[4] *Sayre College et al.* v. *General Assembly of Presbyterian Church of U.S. et al.,* 308 Ky. 404, 214 S.W. 2d 601 (1948).

ready been decided by his predecessor. Thus the order of the probate court was not reviewed or disturbed.[5]

It appears that the City of New York took by condemnation certain real estate from New York University and that a compensatory award of $2,190.22 was confirmed by final decree in 1916, but the university did not claim the award. In 1944 the city paid the amount of the award, with interest, to the state comptroller. Thereafter New York University presented its claim to the state comptroller, who refused payment, relying on the 20-year limitation on the collection of judgments in the Civil Practice Act. The university contended unsuccessfully that the issue should be governed by a section of the Abandoned Property Law which deals with condemnation awards and contains no limitation of such claims. The Appellate Division held that the university's claim was extinguished after the expiration of the first twenty years, and was unaffected by the Abandoned Property Law.[6]

CONDEMNATION PROCEEDINGS MAY BE DROPPED

Wayne University, located in a great metropolis and having housing needs far in excess of the capacity of its current plant, moved to acquire a conveniently located residence-hotel by exercise of eminent domain; but during the pendency of the proceedings the purchase was negotiated by agreement, and the condemnation suit was dropped. Thereupon, some 570 tenants of the building came into court claiming the right to be heard on the question of the public necessity of the purchase. Dismissing this claim, the court curtly asserted the public necessity was clear. Some hardship on the tenants was also clear, but the rights they possessed under contract with the former landlord would not be impaired. The university could lawfully discontinue the

[5] *Denson* v. *Board of Trustees of University of Alabama* (Ala.), 23 So. 2d 714 (1945), later captioned *Ex parte State ex rel. Denson* (Ala.), 26 So. 2d 563 (1946).

[6] *In re Application of New York University*, 271 App. Div. 131, 63 N.Y.S. 2d 556 (1946), *reversing* 185 Misc. 40, 57 N.Y.S. 2d 158 (1945).

condemnation proceedings at any time before confirmation of the verdict of the jury.[7]

MUNICIPAL ZONING AND PRIVATE COLLEGES

Concordia Collegiate Institute, a junior college and preparatory school, has owned its campus in Bronxville, New York, for forty years, far antedating any zoning ordinance. The land is now, however, in a "Residence A" zone, from which educational institutions are excluded by an amendment of 1941, except at the discretion of the zoning board of appeals, and when consents of 80 percent of the neighboring property-owners are shown. In these circumstances the Institute sought a writ of *mandamus* to compel the village superintendent of buildings to disregard the ordinance and issue a permit to erect a building to serve as library, science building, and auditorium. The trial court denied the petition, pointing out that the plaintiff must exhaust its remedies before the village board of zoning appeals before coming into court. Conceding that "A better illustration of 'hardship' than here appears would be hard to find," the court nevertheless declared: "It cannot be said that the exclusion of schools and colleges from a residence zone is so unreasonable as to make the provisions of the ordinance invalid, for it may well be that the residence zone is of such a size and location that it can be adequately served by educational buildings erected beyond its limits." This reasoning seems to take no account of any possible argument for the toleration in residence zones of boardingschools whose students come from a distance and live on the campus.

The judgment was affirmed by the Appellate Division, but the case reached the New York Court of Appeals in 1950, where it was reversed. The unanimous court, in an opinion by Judge Froessel, held the Bronxville zoning amendment of 1941 unconstitutional and invalid, and declared that there is now no limita-

[7] *Hooper* v. *Board of Education of City of Detroit* (Mich.), 23 N.W. 2d 692 (1946).

tion upon the use of the Concordia Collegiate Institute's property for its appropriate educational purposes.[8]

The zoning board of appeals of the town of Oyster Bay granted a variance to permit Long Island University to use certain land in a "Residence A" district "as and for a university with usual campus facilities." When the case reached the Appellate Division, that court, by the narrowly divided vote of three to two, refused to review the action of the zoning board.[9] The two dissenting judges in separate opinions, stressed certain facts in the record: Presiding Judge Lewis thought "The claim of unnecessary hardship is not available to the respondent university, which has merely a conditional contract to purchase the property, and had knowledge of the existence of the zoning regulations." Judge Wenzel agreed that "unnecessary hardship has not been shown," and commented:

> The plight of the owners of the property involved is due to the fact that rural estates and large mansions generally are things of a past era. . . . There is no evidence purporting to show that this is not a general condition in the neighborhood, which may reflect the unreasonableness of the zoning ordinance itself. On the contrary, there is evidence that four other estates have not been sold, though on the market for two to eight years. . . . Further, the advent of hundreds of students in the midst of this area of country estates, and of "usual campus facilities" without circumscription, in my opinion would necessarily alter the essential character of the locality.

LITIGATION REGARDING STATE UNIVERSITY CAMPUSES

A portion of the campus of the State University of Iowa in Iowa City is a tract originally granted by the United States to the territory of Iowa, and never privately owned. It was used as a park from 1839 to 1890, having been so platted in the original plat of Iowa City. A city ordinance of 1890 granted it to the state

[8] *Concordia Collegiate Institute* v. *Miller,* 301 N.Y. 189, 93 N.E. 2d 632 (1950), reversing *Same* (Misc.), 88 N.Y.S. 2d 825 (1949), and (App. Div.), 93 N.Y.S. 2d 922 (1949).

[9] *Hickox et al.,* v. *Griffin et al.,* 274 App. Div. 792, 79 N.Y.S. 2d 193 (1948).

for the use and benefit of the state university, and a subsequent act of the state legislature validated and accepted the grant. A taxpayer's suit was brought in 1948 to quiet title to the ground as a city park, and to declare the ordinance of 1890 and the pertinent statute invalid. The trial court erroneously believed the transfer of 1890 was unconstitutional, but held that the public was estopped from asking rectification after 58 years of apathy. The supreme court of Iowa affirmed the decision as to the result, but on different grounds. In the words of Justice Smith:

> With full realization that there are judicial pronouncements to the contrary, we hold that where land, already publicly owned, is designated for some particular public use, no contractual trust arises in favor of the general public that precludes subsequent diversion of it by proper legislative authority to some other and different public use; at least, where no special private rights have in the meantime arisen by purchase or improvement of adjacent property in reliance on the permanency of the public use in question. . . . We are convinced that there were no constitutional barriers to the transaction in 1890 involving this park.[10]

EASEMENT FOR MUNICIPAL SEWER ACROSS CAMPUS

In 1919 the Ohio State University contracted with the city of Columbus, whereby the university granted an easement for the construction and maintenance of a sewer to be used by both university and city, the university "to use the city sewers on the campus . . . without cost or expense," and to connect with the sewers on the campus without cost. The contract exempted the university from paying any of the expense of construction of the sewer. In 1937 a Columbus city ordinance levied an annual sewer rental charge to pay the expense of treatment and purification of sewage. Doubt existed as to whether the university would be liable for this rental charge, in view of the contract of 1919. In 1947 the legislature appropriated $108,773 to pay the accrued rentals on behalf of the university, provided its liability should be established by the supreme court. Accordingly the issue was

[10] *Carson* v. *State* (Iowa), 38 N.W. 2d 168 (1949).

litigated, resulting in a decision in favor of the city, and a writ of *mandamus* to compel the university to pay the rentals.

The reasoning of the majority of the court was that if the contract of 1919 were interpreted as bargaining away the future legislative power of the city, then it was *ultra vires* and void to that extent.[11]

Only four of the justices concurred in the judgment. One other concurred in the substantive reasoning but dissented on the ground that *mandamus* was not the proper remedy. Two others dissented on the ground that "this decision leaves the university burdened with a perpetual easement but excuses the city from the performance of the obligations it expressly assumed in return therefor." One of these also questioned the availability of *mandamus* as the remedy, and maintained that the contract of 1919 should be held either valid or void *in toto*. The city, thought he, should not be permitted to retain the benefits but repudiate the burdens of the contract.

CONTROL OF BUSY HIGHWAY TRAVERSING STATE COLLEGE CAMPUS

A confusion as to the jurisdiction of several local authorities is brought to light in the 1950 decision of the Oklahoma supreme court sustaining the order of the local board of county commissioners closing and re-routing two blocks of a heavily traveled north-south highway bisecting the campus of the Oklahoma Agricultural and Mechanical College at Stillwater. Petitions of local freeholders for and against the change were before the board of commissioners, and the change was ordered upon evidence that the highway had 30,000 to 40,000 student-pedestrian crossings daily, and that it was heavily traveled by trucks carrying dangerous cargo, such as gasoline, butane, and explosives. The district court of Payne County vacated the order, whereupon the state legislature enacted a statute authorizing the board of regents of a state educational institution to close and re-

[11] *State ex rel. Gordon* v. *Taylor et al.*, 149 Ohio St. 427, 79 N.E. 2d 127 (1948).

route a highway in these circumstances; the city of Stillwater intervened, claiming that the highway in question was in the city and that neither the county commissioners nor the regents of the college had jurisdiction. The supreme court readily decided unanimously, in an opinion by Justice Gibson, that the order of the county commissioners must be restored. This automatically ruled out the city's claim to jurisdiction, and also rendered it unnecessary for the regents of the college to take any action in the matter under their newly enacted authority.[12]

STATE BORROWING TO FINANCE UNIVERSITY BUILDINGS

A Montana act of 1947 authorized the State Board of Examiners (a fiscal authority) to issue $5,000,000 in bonds for the construction of necessary buildings at the six units of the University of Montana, and to determine the amount and date of separate issues within that total. The act was submitted to popular referendum at the general election of November 2, 1948, and approved by a majority of those voting on the question. Election clerks and judges permitted only *property taxpayers* to vote on this question. This was correct, said the Montana supreme court, because although Article XIII, Section 2, of the constitution requires that the creation of an indebtedness exceeding $100,000 shall be submitted to "the people," this is qualified and controlled by Article IX, Section 2, which provides that voters on this question must be taxpayers.

The statute directed a tax levy sufficient to pay the interest and amortization of the debt, but not to exceed two and one-half mills per annum. There was evidence that one mill was sufficient to meet these requirements at the time. It was argued (1) that the legislature could not delegate the computation of the annual rate, and (2) that the maximum of two and one-half mills might at some time in the future be insufficient for the purpose. The court concluded that it is proper for the legislature to impose the duty of computing the exact amount of

12 *Stuart et al.* v. *King et al.* (Okla.), 217 P. 2d 540 (1950).

the levy upon an administrative agency; and that the conjectural question of possible future insufficiently is a matter of policy for the legislature and not a question of law for the court. Hence a writ of injunction to halt the proceedings was refused, and the transaction approved.[13]

[13] *Thomas* v. *Board of Examiners of State* (Mont.), 207 P. 2d 553 (1949).

CHAPTER XX

SELF-LIQUIDATING BUILDING PROJECTS AT STATE INSTITUTIONS

THE trickle of cases wherein the courts approve issues of bonds for the financing of self-liquidating buildings on state college and university campuses continues. There is little that is new and striking in the recent decisions, unless it be the statutory authorization and judicial approval in Oklahoma of the practice of charging student fees for water, heat, and power on the campus, thus putting these utilities into the self-liquidating category.

STATUTORY AUTHORIZATION NOT NECESSARY FOR UNIVERSITY OF MISSOURI

In nearly all instances a state statute specifically authorizing self-liquidating building projects has been regarded as essential, and many of the cases have turned upon questions of exact compliance with the statutes. A Missouri decision of 1946 concerning the University of Missouri is therefore significant, because the state supreme court validated a proposed issue of $2,732,000 dormitory bonds without any authorizing statute at all. The bonds were "payable solely out of the income of said dormitories and dining-room facilities." Keenly aware of the campus-housing stringency, the court said, "Chiefly because of postwar conditions the enrollment at the university will jump from a low of 1,938 students in 1943 to an estimated 6,600 in the fall of this year and then to an estimated 8,000 or more each year for the next decade," and pointed out that the capacity of existing dormitories was only 158 men and 158 women and that many married veterans were living in auto-trailers. The bond issue would finance half the cost of projected dormitories at Columbia for 1,850 men, 550 women, and 250 married veterans; and for 300 men at the school of mines at Rolla. "The curators state they have no express power to issue revenue bonds for money borrowed. Have they the implied power? We are convinced they have in this instance." [1]

OKLAHOMA CASES

The Oklahoma supreme court approved a $325,000 issue of bonds payable "solely from the revenues to be derived from the operation of the buildings," as authorized by a statute of 1945, for the purpose of converting barracks into apartments for veterans at the state agricultural and mechanical colleges. The transaction was not affected by the constitutional limit on state indebtedness because that applies only to obligations for the payment of which resort might be had to the taxing power.[2] The same court refused to approve the issue of $1,300,000 dormitory bonds and $100,000 music-building bonds by the University of Oklahoma because these bonds bore an additional recital: "and in the event of a deficiency in such revenues, then from fees sufficient to make up such deficiency, to be imposed on all students at the University of Oklahoma." This was fatal because it plainly exceeded the intent and wording of the authorizing statute, which, on account of the fact that it was a special act, here took precedence over the general statutory power of the regents of the university to charge fees.[3]

HEATING AND POWER PLANT FOR STATE UNIVERSITY

In 1948 the regents of the University of Oklahoma issued bonds aggregating $1,800,000 to construct a complete heating

[1] *Curators of University of Missouri* v. *McReynolds* (Mo.), 193 S.W. 2d 611 (1946).

[2] *Application of Board of Regents for Oklahoma Agricultural and Mechanical Colleges* (Okla.), 167 P. 2d 883 (1946).

[3] *Application of Board of Regents of University of Oklahoma* (Okla.), 171 P. 2d 597 (1946).

and power plant for the entire university. The bonds are payable only out of the fund to be created by the assessment and collection of student fees, plus certain anticipated net earnings of the power plant, and thus conform to the "special fund doctrine" and create no debt against the state or the university.

A legislative act of 1947 was evidently intended to authorize the transaction specifically, but the validity of the bonds was doubted by two dissenting justices of the state supreme court, though no private party questioned it.

The difficulty resulted from the complexity of the resolution of the board of regents, caused by the fact that provisions for payment of costs of maintenance, insurance, replacements, repairs and extensions, as well as operation of the heating and power plant, were commingled with the provisions for the payment of principal and interest on the bonds issued for its construction.

Fees charged for services to auxiliary enterprises of the university may be applied to insurance, replacements, and repairs of the utility, and there is provision that if all the sources of income heretofore mentioned are insufficient, the regents may in their discretion apply state-appropriated funds toward maintenance and operation; or if not, they may in their discretion charge an additional student fee for that purpose.

In the view of the chief justice and three of his colleagues, constituting a majority of the court, the arrangement for payment of the bonds may be considered to be cleanly separated from the matters relating to operation and other current expenses, and, thus considered, the bond issue unquestionably meets all requirements of the law and is valid. But in the view of the two dissenting justices, the clean separation is not possible because the operating income of the utility is mentioned as one contingent source of the fund for the payment of the bonds, and there is provision for possible application of state funds to the cost of operation; hence in a somewhat remote and indirect sense it could be said the bonds amount in part to a pledging of state funds.

The dissenters admitted that they did not know precisely what was meant by "auxiliary enterprises of the university," but remarked that if such enterprises were sustained out of state revenues, then charges against them would be in effect another contribution of state funds to the income from the operation of the utility.

As a matter of fact, auxiliary enterprises are usually understood to include dining halls, bookstores, and a variety of similar undertakings catering to the convenience of students and faculty, usually operated on a non-profit basis and sustained by charges to their patrons, most of whom are students. Thus the prospective service charges for light and power to the auxiliary enterprises will probably merely amount to an added indirect charge to the students and will not involve any use of state revenues, as feared by the dissenting minority of the court.

A subsidiary issue that was also viewed differently by the two groups of justices may be stated as follows: Conceding that the students of the university may be charged fees for university heating and power when the plant is completed and in operation, can these fees be properly charged to students in attendance at the university during the period of an estimated eighteen months between the issuance of the bonds and the completion of the plant? In other words, can students now in attendance be charged the fee for a service which they are not now receiving and which some of them will never receive?

The majority of the court considered the question and decided that the charge is legitimate, because in all bond-financed undertakings a timely beginning of the stipulated method of collecting the fund for payment of the bonds is essential.

Conceding that the case is not the same as where bonds are to be paid out of taxes, the court remarked that it is the general practice to begin the levy of the specified taxes promptly upon the issuance of the bonds, and before the taxpayers have any opportunity to use or benefit from the structure financed by the bonds.

Thus the University of Oklahoma bond issue is judicially approved by the state's highest tribunal.[4] Whether it is socially wise in the long run to put a university heating and power plant into the self-liquidating category by charging student fees for heat and power is an open question.

UTILITY SYSTEM FOR STATE COLLEGE

In the same year the Oklahoma court approved a $3,000,000 bond issue "for the purpose of construction and extension of a utility plant and system for supplying water, power and heat to the Oklahoma Agricultural and Mechanical College" at Stillwater. Revenues for the amortization of the debt were to be derived from (1) a fee charged every student in regular or summer sessions for the use or availability of the system, and (2) income from the sale of the products and services of the system (such sales to be made only when a surplus above the needs of the college exists). The authorizing statute stipulated that the utility plant should be "of a size and capacity not in excess of the present and reasonably contemplated future needs of the institution." This latter point was the controverted issue within the court, and resulted in another decision by a division of the court, in this instance six justices against three. The dissenters noted that there was in evidence a proposed contract with the city of Stillwater whereby the city would agree to pay the college a minimum of $76,000 annually for water service, and make a demand for water not exceeding a maximum of 6,000,000 gallons per day. This contract was for a term of 25 years, with renewal provisions. There was also evidence that the city intended to close its own water plant, but keep it intact for emergencies. These facts, thought the three dissenting justices, showed an

[4] *Application of Board of Regents of University of Oklahoma* (Okla.), 195 P. 2d 936 (1948).

obvious intent to provide capacity greater than the needs of the college for a long time to come. The majority of the court, however, was unmoved by this argument, and held that the issuing of the bonds was in strict accord with the statutory authorization, and must be approved.[5]

ARKANSAS CASES

In 1947 the board of trustees of the University of Arkansas prepared an issue of bonds in the sum of $400,000 for the construction of two dormitory buildings, under authorization of a statute of 1947. A taxpayer sought an injunction to restrain the issue, pointing to a clause of the state constitution which forbids pledging the faith and credit of the state or any of its revenues "except by and with the consent of the majority of the qualified electors of the state voting on the question at a general or special election." The statute of 1947, he argued, provided for no submission of the question to popular vote, and was therefore unconstitutional. The trial court dismissed this petition, and the supreme court of Arkansas affirmed the dismissal and approved the bonds. Chief Justice Griffin Smith dissented without placing any opinion in the record.

Patiently reiterating the "special fund" doctrine, as has been done before by many courts in many states, the majority of the court pointed out that the bonds recited on their face that "in no event shall they be considered a debt for which the faith and credit of the state of Arkansas or any of its revenues are pledged, and no mortgage or lien on the dormitories or any lands or buildings belonging to the state shall be given as security. . . ." The bonds were not to be issued by the state, not to be signed by any state officer, and not to bear the seal of the state. They were to be issued by the university in its own name, and to be payable solely out of rentals derived from the buildings to be financed by the proceeds of their sale. A clearer case of ad-

[5] *Application of Board of Regents of Oklahoma Agricultural and Mechanical Colleges for "Utility System Revenue Bonds, Series 1948"* (Okla.), 200 P. 2d 901 (1948).

herence to the requisites of the well-established "special fund doctrine" would be hard to find.[6]

PLEDGING REVENUES OF ONE PROJECT TO AMORTIZE DEBT OF ANOTHER PROJECT

Under the same Arkansas statute, the Arkansas State College at State College encountered a legal obstacle when, in planning a project to erect twelve faculty residences, it sought to pledge not only the rentals of the twelve dwellings but also to bind itself, if necessary to prevent a default, to use for the purpose any surplus above a specified amount ($9,000) in the fund accruing from the revenues of other buildings earlier constructed as self-liquidating projects. When a taxpayer sued to halt this scheme, the college answered with a demurrer which was sustained by the trial court; but the supreme court reversed the decision and remanded the case with directions to overrule the demurrer and proceed. The authorizing statute of 1947, said the court, empowered the pledging *only* "of the gross tolls, fees, rents, and other charges . . . to be derived as income from the project. . . ."[7]

KANSAS STATE COLLEGE CASE

A Kansas act of 1947 empowered the State Board of Regents to issue bonds to finance self-liquidating dormitory projects. The board prepared an issue to finance dormitories at the Kansas State College of Agriculture and Applied Science at Manhattan. To test the validity of the bonds, the attorney-general brought an action in *quo warranto* to challenge the Regents' right to sell them. The writ was denied and the bonds approved, with only Chief Justice Harvey dissenting without opinion. To the majority of the court it was clear that the bonds would not represent a debt of the state; but even if they did, said Justice Wedell, such a debt would not be prohibited by the constitu-

[6] *Jacobs* v. *Sharp et al.*, 211 Ark. 865, 202 S.W. 2d 964 (1947).

[7] *Wells* v. *Stuck et al.* (Ark.), 215 S.W. 2d 697 (1948).

tion, because debts within the constitutional prohibitions are debts to be paid by a general property tax, and not from funds to be raised in some other manner, as from rentals of dormitories. The court went on to declare that dormitories are essential educational equipment and that exemption of the bonds from taxation does not violate the constitution; the court held devoid of merit numerous other far-fetched arguments against the constitutionality of the statute and the validity of the bond issue.[8]

UTAH STATE AGRICULTURAL COLLEGE

Against the usual contention that a debt of the state was created contrary to the provisions of the state constitution, the Utah supreme court upheld the validity of an issue of $850,000 in bonds by the Utah State Agricultural College to erect and equip a student union building.[9] All the five justices believed the transaction was valid, but their conclusions were expressed in a majority opinion in which three joined, while another concurred in part and another concurred in the result. The latter two justices thought the fact that the bonds were expressly payable only out of income to be derived from the building was sufficient, without going into the question of the degree of autonomy conferred on the college by virtue of the clause of the constitution which confirms and perpetuates the pre-existing powers and franchises of the state university and the state agricultural college. This aspect of the case is discussed in Chapter VII.

[8] *State ex rel. Fatzer* v. *Board of Regents of State of Kansas*, 167 Kan. 587, 207 P. 2d 373 (1949).
[9] *Spence* v. *Utah State Agricultural College* (Utah), 225 P. 2d 18 (1950).

CHAPTER XXI

ACCESSORY EDUCATIONAL CORPORATIONS AND ASSOCIATIONS

INVARIABLY a college or university, whether privately controlled or otherwise, has associated with it a variety of private nonprofit organizations, such as research foundations, alumni associations, scholarship corporations, college fraternities, and other types. Thus at a state university the central public corporation is surrounded by a fringe of private nonprofit corporations and associations.

ATHLETIC ASSOCIATION OPERATING LAUNDRY AND DRY-CLEANING BUSINESS

The charter of the University of Georgia Athletic Association provides that "The said corporation shall have no capital stock. The object of the said corporation is not pecuniary gain by its members, but is to promote the physical and moral welfare of the student body." Certain plaintiffs who were in the laundry and dry-cleaning business in Athens sued to enjoin the operation of any such business by the Association under contract with the Regents of the University System of Georgia. These tradesmen alleged that the Association, operating as a private commercial corporation, was conducting the laundry and dry-cleaning business formerly conducted by the Regents, and using trucks and other property of the state in violation of several cited sections of the state constitution. The Association answered with a demurrer. The trial court sustained the demurrer and dismissed the action, and this judgment was affirmed by the state supreme court. That tribunal held that all issues in the case were *res judicata* by the recent decision in the case of *Villyard et al.* v. *Regents of University System of Georgia,* 204 Ga. 517, 50 S.E. 2d 313 (1948),[1] wherein the right of the Regents to operate a laundry and dry-cleaning service for students and other persons connected with an educational institution under their control was sustained; the court expressly reaffirmed that decision. Quoting the charter of the Athletic Association, the court concluded that it is not a private commercial corporation, but expressly refrained from deciding whether that question would affect the result in this case.[2]

FRATERNITY BUILDING CORPORATION: RESTRICTIVE COVENANT

Does a covenant in a deed, that the land thereby conveyed "shall not be used otherwise than for residence purposes," exclude its use as the site of a college fraternity chapter house? The supreme court of Georgia has answered this question affirmatively in the instance of the Tau Epsilon Phi fraternity at Emory University. Accordingly the court affirmed a decision overruling general and special demurrers set up in answer to a petition for injunction to restrain the use of the property for a fraternity house. It appeared that the fraternity chapter customarily used its house for chapter meetings, initiations, dances, rush parties, and other forms of entertainment; that the first floor housed a store room, numerous radios, and a soft-drink vending machine; and a large neon sign was maintained in front of the house. Said the court:

> Taking as true, for the purpose of the demurrer, the allegations of the petition as to the nature and character of the particular fraternity house here involved, the way and manner in which it is maintained, and the various activities of its members and guests, as described in the petition, we hold that it would constitute a violation of the covenant.[3]

1 Digested *supra* in Chapter VII.

2 *Westbrook et al.* v. *University of Georgia Athletic Association et al.,* 206 Ga. 667, 58 S.E. 2d 428 (1950).

3 *Mu Chapter Building Fund, Inc.,* v. *Henry* (Ga.) 51 S.E. 2d 841, 7 A.L.R. 2d 431 (1949).

ZONING ORDINANCE RELATING TO FRATERNITIES AND SORORITIES

A Salt Lake City ordinance of 1939 stipulates that premises used by a fraternity or sorority, if located within a restricted residential area, must be located "not more than 600 feet from the lands and premises occupied by the institution to which the fraternity or the sorority is an incident." The University of Utah chapter of Phi Kappa Iota fraternity, having acquired a house outside the 600-foot limit, subsequent to 1939 and with knowledge of the ordinance, attacked the constitutionality of the ordinance, alleging it to be unreasonably discriminatory, arbitrary, and capricious. Joining in the action was another plaintiff, the owner of a private home within the 600-foot limit, who alleged that the enforcement of the ordinance created a congestion of traffic which adversely affected the value of his property.

The trial court sustained the ordinance, and this judgment was affirmed by the supreme court of Utah. Chief Justice Pratt pointed out that the 600-foot limit had a reasonable basis, because at the time it was established it included all fraternity premises then existing except a scattered one or two. Zoning always involves drawing boundaries, which may separate premises very similar in type; and it may involve balancing traffic congestion in one area as against hilarity at late hours in another, said he. All these are legislative questions, and the court will not interfere unless an ordinance is manifestly without reasonable foundation.[4]

COSTS OF INCORPORATING FRATERNITY HOUSING ASSOCIATION

Four individuals, desiring to bring into existence a non-profit charitable corporation chiefly for the purpose of providing housing for selected students at Washington University in St. Louis,

[4] *Phi Kappa Iota Fraternity et al.* v. *Salt Lake City* (Utah), 212 P. 2d 177 (1949).

applied to the district court for approval of their proposed articles of incorporation. The court granted the decree of approval *pro forma,* but allowed the $200 compensation of an attorney who had been called in as *amicus curiae* to investigate and advise the court in the matter, to be charged against the incorporators individually. The court of appeals held that this taxing of costs against the individual petitioners was correct, and enforceable by execution.[5]

TAX EXEMPTION OF STUDENT RELIGIOUS AND SOCIAL CENTER

Early in 1942 the two adjoining Roosevelt residences at 47 and 49 East Sixty-Fifth Street, New York City, were sold to the B'nai B'rith Hillel Foundations, Inc., a District of Columbia corporation, the intent being to remodel the houses to form the Sarah Delano Roosevelt Interfaith Memorial House for certain religious and social activities of Protestant, Catholic, and Jewish students at Hunter College of the City of New York. The Hillel corporation took title merely for the interim until a new corporation could be chartered and organized to own and manage the property. During the period of remodeling, the property was not used.

On March 20, 1943, the projected new corporation was chartered by New York legislative act and subsequently the Hillel corporation delivered the deed to it. The activities for which the property was intended were installed and carried on in 1943 and subsequently.

On the question of municipal taxes for the fiscal years 1942–43 and 1943–44, it was held that the right of exemption existed only from and after March 20, 1943, when the new corporation came into existence. No exemption prior to that date could be allowed, for the double reason that the property was not in use for charitable purposes, and the temporary titleholder, though charitable in character, was foreign to the state

[5] *In re Phi Fathers' Educational Association* (Mo. App.), 203 S.E. 2d 885 (1947).

and therefore excluded from the benefit of New York tax exemption laws.[6]

ALUMNAE ASSOCIATION PROPERTY: TAX EXEMPTION

The Alumnae Association of Mt. Sinai Hospital School of Nursing is a non-profit organization which in 1947 acquired an estate in the city of New Rochelle, to be used as a non-profit rest home for nurses of the Mt. Sinai Hospital and the New Rochelle Hospital. The corporate purposes of the Association are "To raise the standard of the Mt. Sinai Training School for Nurses, to promote fellowship between its members for mutual sympathy and encouragement, and to care for the members when ill." These purposes are within the New York tax exemption statute, as are also the purposes of the rest home and the actual use of the rest home, decided the Appellate Division in a 1948 decision ordering the cancellation of the assessment of taxes against the rest home.[7]

PROPERTY OWNED BY AN ACCESSORY CORPORATION FOR BENEFIT OF STATE UNIVERSITY

The Wisconsin University Building Corporation is a non-stock, non-profit corporation, whose members and officers are required to be certain officers and employees of the University of Wisconsin, and exists solely as an agency of the Regents of the University to buy, sell, and otherwise manage real property for the use and benefit of the university. Any net profits from its operations are paid to the Regents for university purposes. It holds title to numerous parcels of property in and around the city of Madison, none of which was acquired except at the request of the Regents with the future expansion of the university and its facilities in view. When in 1949 the city of Madison placed

[6] *Hunter College Student Social Community and Religious Clubs Association* v. *City of New York* (App. Div.), 63 N.Y., S. 2d 337 (1946).

[7] *People ex rel. Alumnae Association of Mt. Sinai Hospital School of Nursing* v. *Rizzardi, Assessor of the City of New Rochelle* (App. Div.), 79 N.Y.S. 2d 245 (1948).

these properties on the tax assessment rolls, on the technical ground that the title was not in the state, the trial court readily determined that the properties are tax-exempt because the title-holder is only an agent of the Board of Regents which is itself an agency of the state, and the properties are held exclusively for the benefit of the state. This judgment was affirmed by the supreme court of Wisconsin in an opinion by Justice Fairchild, in which he found that the real beneficial interest in all the properties belongs to the state.[8]

[8] *State ex rel. Wisconsin University Building Corporation et al.* v. *Bareis, City Clerk* (Wis.), 44 N.W. 2d 259 (1950).

TABLE OF CASES

FEDERAL

UNITED STATES SUPREME COURT

(*Denying certiorari*)

INFERIOR FEDERAL COURTS

DISTRICT OF COLUMBIA

STATE

ALABAMA

ARIZONA

ARKANSAS

1947 Jacobs v. Sharp et al., 174
1947 Lindsay v. White et al., 68
1948 Wells v. Stuck et al., 174
1949 Gipson v. Ingram et al., 89
1949 Ptak v. Jameson, 32

CALIFORNIA

1946 Botts v. Simpson, 54
1946 Canavan v. College of Osteopathic Physicians and Surgeons, 48
1947 In re Reed's Estate: Parker v. Federation of State Societies, 130
1948 In re Fleming's Estate: Kuchel, Controller, v. First National Trust and Savings Bank of San Diego, 44, 112
1950 Davenport et al. v. Davenport Foundation et al., 135

COLORADO

1946 Galiger v. Armstrong, 41
1949 Colorado School of Mines v. Neighbors et al., 51

CONNECTICUT

1950 Breen v. Larson College, 50

DELAWARE

1948 Woodlen v. Brodnax, 42

FLORIDA

1946 Miller et al. v. Flowers, 41

GEORGIA

1948 Regents of University System of Georgia et al. v. Carroll et al., 73
1948 Villyard et al. v. Regents of University System of Georgia, 70, 177
1949 Mu Chapter Building Fund, Inc., v. Henry, 177
1950 Westbrook et al. v. University of Georgia Athletic Association et al., 177

IDAHO

1946 Smith v. University of Idaho, et al., 57
1950 In re Gem State Academy Bakery, 116

ILLINOIS

1945 Murtaugh v. Washington University, 139
1946 American Medical Association v. Board of Review of Department of Labor, 115
1946 Caruthers v. Fisk University, 45
1946 Continental Illinois National Bank and Trust Company of Chicago v. Sever (St. Louis University et al., Interveners), 139
1947 In re Morton's Estate, 110
1947 People ex rel. Tinkoff et al. v. Northwestern University et al., 29
1949 Board of Regents of University of Wisconsin v. State, 112
1950 Moore v. Moyle et al., 154
1950 Stubblefield et al. v. People's Bank of Bloomington et al., 1932

INDIANA

1946 Hulet et al. v. Crawfordsville Trust Company, 129
1947 Bible Institute Colportage Association of Chicago et al. v. St. Joseph Bank and Trust Company et al., 133
1947 Hachet v. Hachet, 14

IOWA

1949 Carson v. State, 164

KANSAS

1946 In re Smith's Estate; Dressler et al. v. Alumni Association of the Kansas State College et al., 136
1947 In re Porter's Estate: Harkrader v. Johnson, 40
1949 State ex rel. Fatzer v. Board of Regents of State of Kansas, 175

KENTUCKY

1946 Broadway and Fourth Avenue Realty Company v. City of Louisville, 97
1946 Comonwealth ex rel. Harper et al. v. Graham et al., 53

INDEX

Bei Fragen zur Produktsicherheit wenden Sie sich bitte an:
If you have any questions regarding product safety,
please contact:

Walter de Gruyter GmbH
Genthiner Straße 13
10785 Berlin
productsafety@degruyterbrill.com